D1559542

BIBLICAL INTERPRETATION

Biblical Interpretation

Theory, Process, and Criteria

Yung Suk Kim

☙PICKWICK *Publications* · Eugene, Oregon

BIBLICAL INTERPRETATION
Theory, Process, and Criteria

Pickwick Publications
An Imprint of Wipf and Stock Publishers
199 W. 8th Ave., Suite 3
Eugene, OR 97401

www.wipfandstock.com

ISBN 13: 978-1-61097-646-6

Cataloging-in-Publication data:

Kim, Yung Suk.

Biblical interpretation: theory, process, and criteria / Yung Suk Kim.

xvi + 106 p.; 23 cm — Includes bibliographical references and index(es).

ISBN 13: 978-1-61097-646-6

1. Bible—Hermeneutics. I. Title.

BS476.K35 2012

Manufactured in the USA.

"Which of these three, do you think, was a neighbor to the man who fell into the hands of the robbers?' He said, 'The one who showed him mercy.' Jesus said to him, 'Go and do likewise.'" (Luke 10:36–7)

"For the whole law is summed up in a single commandment, 'You shall love your neighbor as yourself.'" (Galatians 5:14)

"Love does no wrong to a neighbor; therefore, love is the fulfilling of the law." (Romans 13:10)

Contents

Acknowledgments

This book would not have seen the light of day without a company of supporters, friends, colleagues, and communities around me. My teaching experience here at Samuel DeWitt Proctor School of Theology at Virginia Union University has helped the development of the book. I thank all of my students for their earnest class participation and perseverance from which I have learned how to explore more effective ways of introducing biblical studies. I am also grateful for the support of my Dean, John Kinney, who not only encourages my teaching and research but also presents a unique model of scholarship that is based on a balance between the head and the heart. I also give thanks to Boykin Sanders, a senior faculty member at the School of Theology, who has supported me as a scholar. This book reflects his vision of the true gospel of Jesus that is to be critically studied and boldly preached today so that God's gospel of freedom and justice may advance in the world. I also thank James Harris, a senior faculty member at our school, who reminds me of the role of the Bible in pulpit preaching. I am also indebted to Robert Wafawanaka, my colleague at the School of Theology, who took great pains in reading the entire manuscript and gave me insightful comments. I cannot enumerate all of my colleagues and the staff at the School of Theology who have encouraged my work.

I also give special thanks to Daniel Patte at Vanderbilt University whose scholarly framework of contextual biblical interpretation has been influential to my research and teaching career. His early research on ethical, contextual biblical interpretation formed the basis for the concept of this book. First as a doctoral student at Vanderbilt, and now as a seasoned scholar and teacher in the field, I have had opportunities to work closely with him. This book contains the very spirit of Professor Patte who emphasizes the diversity of interpretation and ethical responsibility that ensues. I am also grateful for Dale Martin at Yale Divinity School, who has read the earliest draft of this book and encouraged me to pursue its publication. I also give many thanks to Greg Carey, my dear friend, at Lancaster Theological Seminary who has read the entire manuscript and provided critical comments and suggestions. I am also very thankful to Carolyn Sharp at Yale Divinity School who has read a part of the manuscript and made substantial comments for revision. I would also like to thank Larry Welborn at Fordham University, whose unqualified trust and support for my scholarship has nurtured me to be the able scholar that I am now. We have maintained enjoyable scholarly conversations that have greatly impacted my research and this book in particular. I cannot miss James Harrison at Wesley Institute in Australia who has been very supportive of my work. I also give special thanks to my dear friend Jon Berquist at Disciples Seminary Foundation who recognized the value of this book early on and encouraged me to pursue publishing. I cannot miss Mitzi Smith at Ashland Theological Seminary in Detroit, and David Odell-Scott at Kent State University who have been very supportive of my scholarly endeavors.

Above all, nothing would have been possible without my family's unwavering support. My wife, Yong-Jeong's dedication and love for the family are beyond comparison. I give a warm round of hugs and love to my daughters, HyeRim, HyeKyung, and HyeIn, for their understanding of my job.

Preface

I see myself as a critical, contextual biblical theologian who distinguishes history from theology while engaging both of them critically from a wide array of interpretive perspectives.[1] Strictly speaking, history is different from theology in the sense that theology has a tendency to claim more than the measurable reality. However, we cannot retrieve the defacto history. Even if we had had a video camera filming everything of a historical event in ancient times, we still would not have had a correct history or meaning of the event because meaning or history is not the sum of recording but the result of interpretation. But this fact does not mean that we have to give up pursuing to know history. We still have to work hard to understand the historical Jesus, using critical studies of the text, archaeology, anthropology, and sociology. No matter how difficult it may be, the truth is that there is a historical Jesus who lived and died.

One may then ask "Can we trust the Gospels for our faith and guidance in our lives?" The answer is a resounding yes. Although we do not have direct access to the historical Jesus through the Gospels, what we can discover is the diversity of early Christian experiences. We learn four portrayals of Jesus, reflected in each of the gospel communities (Mark, Matthew, Luke, and John). Because of the interweaving nature of history and theology, we can hardly separate one from the other. The Gospels contain

1. What I mean by biblical theologian differs from some popular notion where the Bible is used to support a particular theology that governs the whole text and applies universally. My view of biblical theology is situational and constructive; therefore, readers have to critically evaluate and engage the text and the world presupposed by it. There is no singular biblical theology but there are many theological perspectives because in the Bible there are many voices registered through different communities in different times.

both historical memories and early Christian experience about Jesus. The account of the historical Jesus is recollected, narrated, and written down in a form that embeds theology.

In fact, our interpretation hinges on the intersection between history (what really happened) and story (what are accounted). Let us take the example of Matthew's Gospel. We may think of two different historical times: Jesus' (before 30 CE) and Matthew's (85–90 CE). Given these two historical dimensions, there are at least three possibilities of interpretation. First, we make a distinction between Jesus' time and Matthew's time without blending the two together. We read Matthew's story on its own in its particular context. Second, however, since Matthew contains historical memories about Jesus, we still have to read it as part of the historical Jesus story. Third, we may focus on the process of transmission of the Jesus tradition. By exploring the period of oral traditions (30–70 CE), we engage and evaluate the diverse groups of early Christians.

Ultimately, as we see here, interpretation involves the reader, and no historical or literary criticisms function without the reader's engagement with the text. Even in a historical critical approach, it is the reader who decides the final meaning of the text because historical meaning or knowledge also depends on the reader's method or judgment. The reader makes multiple decisions regarding the "selection of which 'things' count as evidence and which may be ignored, the choice of ways to read or interpret the evidence, and the ways in which one may structure an argument."[2] Therefore, strictly speaking, every interpretation is contextual and no interpretation is possible without the reader.[3] Thus, what matters is not simply what the text says but how we know what we know (matters of epistemology). More importantly, we have to take a position in our interpretation. For example, if we conclude that the Lukan community is socially conservative from our studies, it does not mean that our job of

---

2. Email correspondence with Carolyn Sharp, Professor at Yale Divinity School. October 13, 2011.

3. Phyllis Trible, "Authority of the Bible," 2248–60. Trible emphasizes the role of the reader in making biblical authority. I see myself as a critical contextual biblical theologian. While a biblical theologian uses the Bible as a source of theology, often ending up with a harmonious doctrinal reading at the expense of the diversity of biblical writings, my approach to biblical theology critical and contextual. "Critical" means examining biblical writings from a diversity of interpretive perspectives, and "contextual" means considering life contexts of the text and the readers alike.

interpretation is done, because the interpreter should respond to the voice of conservatism in the Gospel of Luke.

With this move to a critical contextual interpretation, I deal with three main questions: What is critical contextual interpretation? What is the process of interpretation? How do we know which interpretation is the most persuasive or compelling in a particular context? I attempt to integrate various theories and strategies of biblical interpretation into a coherent paradigm of critical contextual interpretation, which requires a critical examination of both the text and the reader. I also explore a set of criteria for solid interpretation. My hope is that this small book will invite readers to critically engage in the scriptures by rethinking the role of the Bible in the global world today.

CHAPTER ONE

Introduction

The Need for Critical Contextual Interpretation

The Bible is perhaps the most read book in the world and yet its influence is mixed. People seek the Bible for different reasons or purposes. One group of people looks to the Bible to find biblical authority applicable to their lives today; but even among this group, there are different approaches to analyzing the Bible. Some read the Bible devotionally and apply the lessons to their lives. They do not care much about the historical contexts of the texts, take the stories of the Bible as divinely inspired, and only pick up what they need from the Bible. Others read texts theologically by looking at the historical and literary contexts, usually done through a particular reading lens that aims at a particular theological doctrine. For instance, Paul's letters are read through the lens of "justification by faith" at the price of the deeper and more complex aspects of justice or righteousness language used by Paul.[1]

On the other hand, the other group reads the Bible critically as a historical product like any other historical document.[2] They are more interested in the history and knowledge contained in these ancient texts

1. For Paul's theology, see Yung Suk Kim, *A Theological Introduction to Paul's Letters.*
2. John Barton, *The Nature of Biblical Criticism*, 31–68.

1

2 BIBLICAL INTERPRETATION

than of the present interaction between the texts and the reader. Certainly, this way of reading is important to our understanding of the texts, because otherwise, we may lose some voices of ancient texts, which should not be glossed over by later readers. But even within this area of study, the readers are not purely objective or value free. Though not explicitly, they still have a set agenda in their studies that affect the modern life context. Sexuality is a good example as can be seen in Rom 1:26–27. This passage can be interpreted in various ways, with no absolute verdict on the issue of sexuality.[3] As Dale Martin points out, strictly speaking, texts do not mean, but we mean with texts, because no matter what voice is uncovered or claimed, it is the reader who ultimately decides a particular position.[4] For example, if Paul is considered a misogynist, one can decide whether or not he or she will accept Paul's misogynist position. The meaning of a text is the result of negotiation between the text and the reader, as will be clarified in the reader-oriented approach below.

As we see here, any interpretation of a text, professional or ordinary, involves the reader's choice, which affects not only the immediate readers but also other people. On the one hand, the diversity of interpretation is to be celebrated because the Bible can be read from a variety of perspectives, but on the other hand, it does not mean that all interpretation is good, ethically sound, or helpful to others. The question is how we explain the existence of harmful or naïve interpretation that happens not simply because the reader is ill equipped but because the nature of biblical interpretation is more complex than we think. That is, any interpretation involves at least three layers of difficulties: the text, translation, and interpretation. The first layer is the text itself. We do not have original copies of the Greek or Hebrew texts. What we have are copies of copies of copies of a copy. Therefore, the first task is to establish credible texts among the variant manuscript traditions. The second layer is translation that requires highly technical training in terms of original language. But at the same time any translation is an interpretation. So we have to be careful about translation. The third layer is interpretation that involves the reader. These three layers are not independent of each other. Oftentimes the interpreter's theology influences his or her translation and particular variant reading among others. Although this book primarily deals with matters of interpretation (the third layer), we will briefly see the difficulties involved in each layer.

3. Martin, *Sex and the Single Savior*, 51–76.
4. Ibid., 33.

Matters of Textual Criticism

1 Cor 14:33b–36 is a notoriously debated text not only from a textual critical point of view but also from a theological perspective because this passage often has been understood as rejecting women's place in the church. Since this particular passage is similar to 1 Tim 2:11–15 (written around 90s or latest in 110 CE), it is argued that 1 Cor 14:33b–36 is an interpolation (an inserted text) by later copyists or editors who were interested in gender hierarchy in the church. Given that Paul's letters were written between 50s and 60s, later church leaders or copy editors could add their conservative voice to Paul's texts to make sure that the church follows a gender hierarchy of society. That is what we see a similar kind of conservative tone and message between 1 Cor 14:33b–36 and 1 Tim 2:11–15 (see below):

1 Tim 2:11–15 (NRSV)

> Let a woman learn in silence with full submission. I permit no woman to teach or to have authority over a man; she is to keep silent. For Adam was formed first, then Eve; and Adam was not deceived, but the woman was deceived and became a transgressor. Yet she will be saved through childbearing, provided they continue in faith and love and holiness, with modesty.

1 Cor 14:33–36 (NRSV)

> For God is a God not of disorder but of peace. (As in all the churches of the saints, women should be silent in the churches. For they are not permitted to speak, but should be subordinate, as the law also says. If there is anything they desire to know, let them ask their husbands at home. For it is shameful for a woman to speak in church. Or did the word of God originate with you? Or are you the only ones it has reached?)

We find in 1 Tim 2:11–15 a more rigid tone of women degradation than in 1 Cor 14:33–36; that is perhaps because the community behind this pastoral letter is more rigid in its view of gender than the earlier times. As the church becomes larger and when Christ does not return as quickly as possible for later Christians in the second century CE, understandably, they choose to grow the church by accepting the conventional hierarchical view of gender and society. Accordingly, 1 Tim 2:11–15 says that the reason for women's silence in the church is sought from the story of creation and fall in Genesis (mainly from Gen 2–3 where scholars identify the second account of creation); Eve was formed second after Adam; the implication is that she is subordinate to Adam. Furthermore, Eve was deceived first, and became a transgressor. Otherwise, there is no charge against Adam. But according to the first account of creation in Gen 1, we do not see hierarchy between male and female since both are created at the same time in the image and likeness of God (Gen 1:27). Nevertheless, later Jews and Christians interpret Genesis with a focus on gender hierarchy based on the second account of creation. Likewise, in 1 Tim women's salvation comes through childbearing, which underscores women's particular role of reproduction and domestic work. To a lesser degree, however, there is a similar tone of women degradation in 1 Cor 14:33b–36.

Given the existence of a difficult text such as this (1 Cor 14:33b–36), we have to decide whether this text is Paul's or not. Many people consider this text as an interpolation because except for this particular text, Paul's view of women is positive throughout his letters. He is seen as egalitarian and works with other women leaders such as Phoebe and Priscilla. Junia is named the first woman apostle (Rom 16:7). Women in the Corinthian church are freely participating in worship, praying and prophesying (1 Cor 11:5).[5] The other interpretive option is that Paul wrote these texts. But within this option there are different explanations for it. Whereas some consider Paul a social conservative (not allowing women to speak in the church), others contextualize this text by fitting it into a particular local ministry context. To this latter group, Paul is concerned not with women's place in the church in general, but he is concerned about a particular disruptive practice of some women in the church who may have been related to a mystery religion.[6] There is still another option. That is, 1 Cor 14:33b–36 is considered Paul's text, but he quotes from his rivals and refutes their restraining position on women.[7] In this view, 1 Cor 14: 36 is Paul's rebuttal of their position on women: "Or did the word of God originate with you? Or are you the only ones it has reached?" As we see here, matters of textual criticism involve more than the question of which text is correct or acceptable; rather, they require the reader's critical discernment. There are

5. Kim, *Christ's Body in Corinth*, 90–92. See also Wire, *The Corinthian Women Prophets*, 116–34.

6. Schüssler Fiorenza, *In Memory of Her*, 233.

7. Odell-Scott, "Let the Women Speak in Church," 68–74.

numerous textual issues in the Bible; some are minor or negligible, but others are crucial to our understanding of texts.[8] If there are textual variants, the reader should decide which text he or she will choose. That is actually the start of interpretation.

Matters of Translation

Erga Nomou (Gal 2:16)

The best literal translation of *erga nomou* in Gal 2:16 may be "works of the law." But the old New International Version (NIV) has it: "observing the law," which is not a plain translation. It is a translation from a specific theological interest, based on the doctrine of justification by faith. The idea behind such a translation is based on the legalist view of Judaism in which individual righteousness is obtained through observing the law.[9] No matter how difficult it is to understand the meaning of the "works of the law," the translation should maintain the original syntax, which is close to literal equivalence translation. Generally speaking, NRSV is close to literal equivalence, whereas NIV to dynamic equivalence, according to which word-for-word translation is not maintained.

Because of this, dynamic equivalence translation should be discouraged because it does not give full attention to original wording or syntax. What we have here are the two nouns (works and law), which are combined through the Greek genitive case. Indeed, the Greek genitive relationship is complex and often ambiguous. A simple example comes from *dikaiosyne theou*, "the righteousness of God" (Rom 1:17; 3:21–26). It can mean God's righteousness (the subjective genitive) or individual righteousness coming from God (the objective genitive).

The difference between the subjective and the objective genitive cases is like the distance between heaven and earth. If we take this phrase *dikaiosyne theou* as the subjective genitive, it is God's righteousness: it is the God who is righteous and loving. In the objective genitive ("a righteousness coming from God," as translated in the NIV), the emphasis is on individual

---

8. For a brief overview of manuscript traditions, see Soulen, *Sacred Scripture,* 29–44. Regarding textual issues of the New Testament, see Metzger and Ehrman, *The Text of the New Testament.* For textual criticism of the Hebrew Bible, see Emanuel Tov, *Textual Criticism of the Hebrew Bible.* See also Gary Martin, *Multiple Originals.*

9. For more about this phrase *erga nomou*, see Yung Suk Kim, *A Theological Introduction to Paul's Letters,* 20–22.

righteousness. Here God is the source of righteousness rather than an actor of righteousness, as we saw in the subjective genitive case. Similarly, if we think of "the works of the law," the relationship between works and the law should still be reflected in the translation and not be explained away.

Therefore, we cannot ignore the original syntax of the phrase (Greek genitive) because the phrase may mean something other than what it is commonly interpreted as. In this case, "works of the law" can mean a particular practice of the law (i.e., circumcision) imposed on Gentile Christians in the Galatians context. The issue may not be about the whole law *per se* but a particular attitude toward the law in people's lives (i.e., zeal for the law or ethnic particularism). In fact, As E. P. Sanders argues, Judaism in the first century CE was not a legalistic religion.[10] Paul actually affirms the place of Israel and of the law: "So the law is holy, and the commandment is holy and just and good" (Rom 7:12). "I ask, then, has God rejected his people? By no means! I myself am an Israelite, a descendant of Abraham, a member of the tribe of Benjamin. God has not rejected his people whom he foreknew" (Rom 11:1–2). In this regard, Paul continues Jesus' spirit and attitude toward Jewish law, as Jesus says: "I came not to destroy the law but to fulfill it" (Matt 5:17).[11]

Katalambano (John 1:5)

The best translation of *katalambano* in John 1:5 may be "to overcome" (NRSV) or "to seize." But the NIV (old version) has it as "to understand."[12] The difference between "to overcome" and "to understand" is not too small to ignore. The most plain sense of *katalambano* is "to make something one's own, to gain control of someone through pursuit (seize)."[13] If darkness connotes many meanings such as corrupt people, evil in (of) the world, and evil force or Satan, the meaning of *katalambano* has to be inclusive of many connotations of darkness. Therefore, "to overcome" is better than "to understand." But the NIV translation reduces the diversity of connotation of darkness to matters of "understanding," and the implication is that the

10. Sanders, *Paul and Palestinian Judaism*, 552.

11. For a brief overview of translation of biblical texts, see Soulen, *Sacred Scripture*, 45–59.

12. In this book I am using the previous version of the NIV (1984). There is a new version released in 2011.

13. Danker, *Greek English Lexicon of the New Testament*, 519–20.

truth (or the light) has to do with "understanding." With this reductionism, darkness refers to unbelieving humans who do not "understand" who Jesus is, and salvation means accepting Jesus as a personal savior who paid the price for people's sins.

Certainly, this translation is plausible, but the problem is, by limiting the connotation of *katalambano* to "understanding," the broad context of darkness it stands for is omitted. However, the NRSV translates it as "to overcome," which is more accurate than the NIV, because now darkness symbolizes more than the human cognitive area. It points to a variety of forces of darkness, human or non-human. The darkness connotes all spheres of life that block the light of the Logos. The believer's task is not merely to believe or understand the Logos but to follow Jesus as the Logos who embodied God's presence in the world at all costs.

Matters of Interpretation

Interpretation means explaining a text from a wide array of perspectives. If we follow this line of thought, all interpretation is contextual. Suppose we have a secure text with a good translation, we still have to explain the text (meaning) because meaning is understood differently depending on different textual (interpretive) approaches. The complexity of interpretation comes from both the text and the reader, and we are led to answer these following questions when we deal with any texts: How, why, and what do we read? The question of "how" deals with a text, the question of "why" with contextuality of the text and the reader, and the question of "what" with the theological lens of texts and the reader. All these questions and issues regarding interpretation can be expressed in the following statement: "We are reading the Bible." *We* corresponds to the reader, *are reading* to the theological lens, and *the Bible* to texts. The Bible can be read variously, as history, theology, and literature. Readers read texts for a purpose (that is, the question of why we read). The theological lens (interchangeable with "engagement" in this book) refers to a particular theological choice, which usually involves theological concept or view of text. For instance, theological concepts of "the cross of Jesus" are varied and should be deliberated to decide which concept of the cross works. View of text refers to the role of scripture; for example, the role of good news, or the role of correcting crooked discipleship. We will come back to this issue in later chapters.

To show why interpretation matters and how these three elements of interpretation (the reader, the theological lens, and the text) operate, we will take John 14:6 as an example: "I am the way, the truth, and the life; nobody comes to the Father except through me." What does this text mean to John's community or to us today? The interpretive keys are many and beg the answer for the following questions: What is the way? What is the truth or the life? To understand this text, should we look to a historical Jesus or depend on the reconstruction of the Johannine community? Below there are a few possible readings that involve three elements of interpretation.

The Way to Heaven

"The way to heaven" means that Jesus saves and leads people to heaven, providing believers with immortal (eternal) life. Jesus paved the way to God by dying for sinners. A soul's going to heaven is the ultimate goal and meaning of life in this world. In this reading, the need of the reader has to do with a secure identity in Christ, being saved from this world. The way to heaven is a new life beyond this world. That is the theological concept of the way. This view of the text (role of the text) is to provide knowledge through which the reader is assured about his or her identity in the future. Textual approach is literary, reading the theological story/journey of Jesus who paves the way to heaven. While this reading is possible, it is unlikely that Jesus acts like Gnostic Christians who emphasize the way (knowledge) to heaven.

An Exemplary Life

"An exemplary life" means that Jesus' work provides the sense of "I-am sayings" in John 14:6. Jesus is the way because he worked the way as the Son of God. Jesus is the truth because he testified to it. Jesus is the life because he showed us how to live according to the will of the Father. Jesus worked to bring the life and the light to the world. Jesus' teaching is not about the otherworldly salvation but about what to do for God right now. The gist of his teaching is sacrifice for others. Jesus asks believers and others to eat his flesh and drink his blood (John 6:54–55). Jesus here does not institute Eucharist, as opposed to in the synoptic Gospels, but talks about a theology of sacrifice, which is accomplished through an actual life of living for others.[14] Eating his flesh and drinking his blood stands for the life of sacrifice that includes the whole life of Jesus. Thus his teaching is difficult, as his disciples wonder (John 6:60). The climax of Jesus' life or ministry in John's Gospel does not end up with the cross. Rather, in the Prologue Jesus is the Logos incarnate and meets opposition from people because of his message and action about the Logos whose purpose is to provide the life and the light to the world. In other words, his whole life is a life of sacrifice for God and others.

This reading also involves the reader's choices. The need of the reader here is an exemplary model or figure to follow so that he or she can know how to live in an unjust, selfish world and how to secure justice. The implication is that the believers also have to follow Jesus who is the way for others. This view of the text is an "empowering word" through which the believers may live boldly in the face of difficulties of life in the world. The theological concept of "way" has to do with the moral transformation that involves personal change of heart and socio-political change in society. In terms of textual approach, Jesus' earthly ministry (the historical dimension) is read through his kingdom message of the way narrated in the Fourth Gospel (the literary dimension).

A Particular Message to the Johannine Community

This reading focuses on the Johannine community's historical situation and need. The way of Jesus has to do with the way Jesus provides comforting words to the struggling community that experiences a recent split from the synagogue. John 14:1 reflects the emotional status of separation: "Do not be troubled in your heart, because there are many dwelling places in my father's house." The main reason for the split is Christological (the view of Messiah), and this community believes that Jesus is the Jewish messiah. "I am the way" is the message of assurance that the members of the

14. I am not aware of any scholarly literature that emphasizes this kind of sacrificial theology, as I understand. Eating Jesus' flesh means participating in his life and death, as he shows a radical love of God through his body. Those who are born from above (the Spirit) can participate in Christ. In this respect, Paul's body metaphor, the body of Christ (*soma christou*) in 1 Corinthians can be understood as Christ's own body, his life and death. Derivatively, then, we can think of the believer's radical participation in Christ ("You are Christ's body" means "you are Christ-like body"). See Yung Suk Kim, *Christ's Body in Corinth*, 65–95.

community made the right choice. So the message goes like this: "Don't worry about your future. I am the way to you. If you abide in me, you are in God the Father. Your place in the Johannine community is a good one." In this reading, the need of the reader is to secure one's identity in God. The concept of the way has to do with personal assurance about the messiah (Christology). This view of the text is an "empowering word" for downtrodden people who experienced a recent split. The primary textual approach here is historical and sociological. The historical Johannine community is investigated from a sociological or social scientific approach (using sect theory or legitimation theory).[15]

The Way of Jesus as Embodiment of God's Love

The other possible reading of the way is more inclusive than all the above readings. This reading emphasizes Jesus' obedience to God and his embodiment of God's love. Jesus is not equal with God. Jesus prays to God, works for God, and always acknowledges God as the one who sent him to the world to bring the life and the light. He is the Son of God who shows who God is through his life and death. His death is the cost of preaching and living for the way of God, which is liberation and life. What he emphasizes is not equality, but union with God. The son shows God's love. That is what one means. Actually, the gender of "one" in Greek (John 10:30) is not masculine (*heis*) but neuter (*hen*), which suggests the idea of unity.

In this reading, therefore, the name of Jesus and his work should cohere. Put differently, the name of Jesus is not the same as the Logos, the way, the truth or the life. Jesus is the way, the truth, and the life precisely because he showed them (the way, the truth, and the life) through his life and death. He is an incarnation of God. To follow the way of Jesus, the life of Jesus, and the truth of Jesus, requires living and dying like him. It is not like saying "my way is a secure highway because Jesus has done all for me or he has been punished instead of me." Rather, the true life means the true sacrifice; the way means the way of sacrifice. Even Jesus' last saying on the cross – "all was finished" (John 19:28) may not mean that he completed all

15. In the 1970s–80s the social scientific approach (social history included) to the Bible had been influential and still a good number of followers stay in that paradigm. John's Gospel was considered a sectarian community who sets itself against others (in this case, the synagogues). For a trend in this study in general, see Meeks, *The First Urban Christians*. Theissen, *The Sociology of Early Palestinian Christianity*. For John's Gospel in particular, see Meeks, "The Man from Heaven in Johannine Sectarianism."

salvific works so that there are no human works required. But this saying means in this context that Jesus finished his due work as the messiah. That is, Jesus as the Son of God showed the way of life (not liberation from evil or darkness), the way of love and sacrifice for God and neighbors, and the way of truth in the midst of so many crooked hearts and the corrupt political powers.

So ultimately, the way that Jesus discusses is not the knowledge or the gate to heaven but a life of love and sacrifice for God and the disciples. The incarnate Son of God showed the light and the life to the world, but the world (representing the power of darkness) did not accept it because of fear that their evil acts would be exposed to the light (John 3:19–24). Jesus did not give in to this opposition but walked the way of love and justice. That is his obedience to the Father. The Father and Son are one in unity. It is the unity of a loving relationship. That is what Jesus asks his disciples and Jews to continue in his word. If they abide in his word, they are truly his disciples (John 8:31). His word is the life of love and sacrifice for others. The way of God is lived through Jesus, and continues to be lived through his disciples.

In this reading, the reader's need may be holistic transformation that involves self, God, and the neighbor. As Jesus walked his way for transforming the world, the believers need to follow the way of Jesus, imitating his bold faith and deep love for God and their neighbor. The concept of the way here is holistic and involves many aspects of the way: knowledge, motivation, sacrifice, and God's love. The view of the text is like wearing "corrective glasses" through which the believers see the world and humanity differently, or through the way of Jesus (his life and death) that embodies God's presence. The primary textual approach here is historical and literary. The Johannine community is in view and the story of the Fourth Gospel is read through the story of Jesus who embodies God's love in the world.

Summary

In this chapter we have seen that biblical interpretation involves three layers of difficulties (the text, translation, and interpretation) and three elements of interpretation (the text, the reader, and the theological lens). There are complexities and diversity of biblical interpretation; however, not all readings are equally valid or helpful. Therefore, it is crucial to explain and compare different readings with each other. All in all, the ultimate question is which interpretation is better than the other and how do we know? For this goal of exploring and evaluating complex biblical interpretation, Chapter 2 discusses the text (textuality). The question here is how do we approach the text? Chapter 3 deals with the reader (contextuality), and the primary question here is who reads the text and why? Chapter 4 discusses the process of interpretation by focusing on the reader, the text and the theological lens. Here the main question is how particular meaning is focused and chosen by the reader. Also, the focal point here is to see how the process of complex interpretation works. Then, Chapter 5 discusses criteria for solid interpretation. The question is how do we evaluate various interpretations? Chapter 6 discusses "the kingdom of God" as a test case of critical contextual interpretation. Then, the conclusion follows in Chapter 7.

Questions for Further Reflection

1. What is biblical authority? How do we know which authority we should follow? Who decides?

2. What is the relation between the Hebrew Scriptures and the New Testament? Is there continuity or discontinuity between them? Explain in each case.

3. What is textual criticism? Why are there so many variant readings in manuscript traditions? What do they reveal?

4. Why does translation matter? Compare the following texts of the two translation versions (NRSV and NIV): Rom 3:21–26. What are major differences between these two versions? On other occasions, translation of a particular word (Greek or Hebrew) is critical. Look at the following Greek words and compare the translation of each word in different English versions: *erga nomou* (Gal 2:16) and *katalambano* (John 1:5).

5. Why does interpretation matter? What is the role of the reader? Explain the importance of interpretation using *erga nomou* (Gal 2:16).

6. Using John 14:6 ("I am the way"), discuss various ways of interpreting "the way." What are the three elements of interpretation?

CHAPTER TWO

Textuality: *How* Do We Read?

In this chapter and the following two chapters, we will explore a process of contextual interpretation that involves the text (Chapter 2), the reader (Chapter 3), and engagement (Chapter 4). Textuality refers to and concerns all aspects of the text—written or oral. Written text involves inter-texts and various other contexts. Sometimes, the more important thing is not just what is written there before us, but what is left out of the text. For example, some women's voices did not make it into the sacred books of the Bible.[1] Attention should be given not only to what was said but what was not said. Eventually, the most important question we have to ask about textuality is: "Whose text is it?"[2] Subsequently, more related questions arise: Who wrote or edited the text? Why was it written or edited? How have these texts been read within the historical community behind them or throughout the history of the church? Before examining methods of the text, it is worth investigating the nature of the Bible.

---

1. For instance, the so-called Pastoral Epistles reflect a male hierarchical voice while suppressing women's voices in the church. Moreover, some books of the Hebrew Bible are also understood as reflecting a male elite voice (1–2 Kings could be a case, where Davidic kings are legitimated at the expense of ordinary people).

2. Sakenfeld, "Whose Text is It?" 5–18.

What Is the Bible?[3]

It is true that the Bible, in whole or in part, has functioned as sacred scripture for both historical communities lying behind the texts, that is, for Judaism and Christianity, and for Jews and Christians throughout history.[4] For some scholars, however, the Bible is no more than a collection of ancient texts that contain diverse religious (or political) experiences of people in the ancient past. For a heuristic purpose, we need to make a distinction between the text of the Bible and its function as scripture. The former is a record of ancient cultures and religious experiences, and the latter is a result of interpretation that affects the readers in a community.

While this distinction is arbitrary or ambiguous, it has merit because each of these can be evaluated separately. That is, reading the Bible involves a deliberate process of scriptural discernment, and the question is: In what sense is the portion of the Bible (or as a whole) scripture? Indeed, in a critical reading of the text, not all voices in the Bible are transformative or helpful to our lives today, as feminist interpreters point out to an androcentric, elite view of the text.[5] The Bible becomes scripture, partially or as a whole, not because of what is simply written there (in the sense of literalism, Biblicism, or biblical inerrancy), but because the reader discerns what is good and acceptable to God and their neighbors. This discernment is possible when the reader critically engages texts in view of their reading lens and life context.[6] In that way, the Bible is deemed authoritative and functions as scripture, and the power of God is channeled through an ongoing interpretation of the Bible in diverse, life changing contexts today.[7]

More than that, the distinction between the text of the Bible and scripture manifests itself if we take the composition of the Bible seriously. The Bible is a collection of ancient texts that contain diverse religious (or

3. Much of this section was published in my initial article for the *Journal of Bible and Human Transformation:* "Rationale and Proposal."

4. The so-called canonical criticism looks into the nature or development of canon within each community behind the specific writing(s) in the Bible. For example, see Morgan, *Between Text and Community,* 1–29.

5. The widely read commentary on women and the Bible is *Women's Bible Commentary* in which androcentric viewing lenses and interests are pointed out. See also Tamez, "Women's Rereading of the Bible," 48–57.

6. Tracy, "Theological Interpretation of the Bible Today," 167–80. In contrast, N. T. Wright does not emphasize the critical role of the reader. See *Scripture and the Authority of God,* 1–45.

7. Trible, "Authority of the Bible."

political) experiences of people in the ancient past. The Bible is not a single book with one grand meta-narrative. Rather, it is composed of many books of different genres, written and rewritten, interpreted and reinterpreted, in different times and places, and thus contains many views or theologies. It is an historical product of different times and places where divergent audiences (as readers) play crucial roles in shaping the traditions or writings of the Bible. So if there are many views in the Bible, there are also many roles of text. Ultimately, the task of the interpreter is to discern what is good and acceptable to God and to our neighbor. This is a process of scriptural reasoning through which we encounter a variety of views or voices in the text and in history.[8]

Here we come to realize the double character of the Bible: sacred text and historical writing. While I reject Biblicism or fundamentalism because they deny the multiplicity and complexity of the Bible, I recognize the value of theological interpretation that makes a connection between the Bible and the reader today. As Dale Martin shows, premodern theologians such as Augustine practiced theological interpretation of scripture.[9] Martin is right when he claims that historical critical methods do not serve theological interpretation of scripture if they disregard the purpose of studying the Bible in a religious, theological setting. On the other hand, while it is important to read the Bible as sacred scripture, making a close connection between the texts and our lives today, I still believe that it is necessary to distinguish the Bible (as written texts) from scripture, because such a distinction helps us appreciate the diversity of vivid historical memories and events behind divergent writings of the Bible, without easily harmonizing different voices or reducing to a single metanarrative.

This kind of diversity in the Bible is both a challenge and a blessing to us; it is a blessing because the difference in traditions reflected in the texts helps us to see the diversity of life experiences in "readers in particular historical contexts" (in that sense, this is a blessing).[10] It is also a challenge because we have to discern what is good, given the unstable, historical document. For example, seemingly contradicting creation stories in Gen 1–2 testify to the existence of multiple voices in the texts, voicing different views about God, and at the same time challenging us, as I have stated elsewhere:

8. Smith, *What is Scripture?* 212–42.
9. Martin, *Pedagogy of the Bible,* 1–45.
10. Sharp, *Wrestling the Word,* 5.

P's inclusion of such a different story (in this case, a creation account) has to do with: (a) rearranging materials for P's cause: order, cosmos, covenant, etc., so that other stories serve P; (b) honoring available traditions because there were different voices in the community; and (c) appreciating the different aspects of God that complement P's view of God. But the bottom line is that, for whatever reason, there are, undeniably, multiple traditions that we can trace back to earlier times when they were first started. Hopefully, we can study a process of tradition changes over time. In this way, we can have a glimpse of how/what each community lived for. We may understand better how each community, though limited, lived faithfully in their time. In this process, we also see ideological elements, good and bad, at work in each community.[11]

Therefore, it is important that we read a text critically and faithfully in view of its diversity and complexity. We also acknowledge that there is an unbridgeable gap between the text and the reader. From a historical critical perspective, what is written in the text is less than what is out there either in the author's mind or in society. So the text does not fully reflect the author or society through the text. From a literary perspective, what is written in the text tells more than what the author intends to say, because the literary product is viewed as independent from the author. So in this view, ironically, the text is greater than the author's intention. From a reader-critical perspective, still complex is that the text can be either bigger than the reader or smaller than it in the sense that what is written there in the text has effective power to readers (so readers are absorbed in the text), or in the sense that what is written there does not fully reflect the world of readers. This gets into the question of intertextuality; that is, the hearer/reader brings to the text all other related texts known by the hearer/reader.

Because of this kind of complexity involved in our interpretation, there is a holy, even mystical chasm between the text and the reader; so let it go like a forever running river, which runs all the way to the sea, with detours and meanderings. Yet the goal of the river is to provide a source of life for the people around it. So our interpretation of the Bible, like an ever-flowing river, provides a rich source of life for all only when we engage it through a critical, creative lens locked in human transformation.

11. Kim, "A Lesson from Studies of Source Criticism."

Approaches to the Text

Historical-critical Approach: "Meaning behind the Text"

A first approach to the text is the Enlightenment-driven historical-critical approach where the texts are treated as historical products (like excavating ancient remains under the ground).[12] Here the text serves as a "window" to the world it refers to, and the traditional historical-critical criticisms engage the text for that purpose: source criticism, form criticism, redaction criticism, and tradition-history criticism. These criticisms concern historical realities of the people and communities behind the text. On the other hand, rhetorical criticism and social scientific criticism examine socially conditioned realities of people in communities.[13] Whereas rhetorical criticism's goal is to reconstruct the rhetorical situation and the strategy, social scientific criticism aims to reconstruct the social world of the text.[14] In this historical-critical approach (socio-rhetorical approach included), interpreters think that they can distance themselves from their social location or life experiences. This approach is good to the extent that we honor the texts in their social historical setting, without willy-nilly reading into the text. However, the weaknesses of these approaches to the text are: 1) there is no engagement between the text and the reader; 2) there is a tendency of neglecting the interpreter's life context; 3) there is also a tendency toward literalism, if anyone claims that the historical theological meaning is the only meaning of the text.[15]

Literary Approach: "Meaning within the Text"

A second approach to the text is literary criticism, such as structural criticism or narrative criticism, which contends that the meaning of a text is independent of its historical context, is constructed within the text, apart

12. The diverse ways of understanding the text is well explained by Sandra M. Schneiders. See *The Revelatory Text*, 113–28. For a diversity of interpretation, see McKenzie and Haynes, ed. *To Each Its Own Meaning*. See also Clark-Soles, *Engaging the Word*, 13–34.

13. Martin, "Social-scientific Criticism," 125–41.

14. Kennedy, *New Testament Interpretation through Rhetorical Criticism*, 3–38.

15. Collins, *The Bible after Babel*, 1–25.

from the historical investigation of the text.[16] The text here primarily serves as a medium that communicates certain religious messages to the reader. So who wrote the text is not directly important to interpretation; the author is assumed in the reading of the text but not investigated as in a historical critical approach. Whereas historians search for the past, theologians or readers in these approaches find meaning in linguistic structures, or cultural structures encapsulated in language, some of which may be concerning religious beliefs, values, etc. In this way the text is liberated from the grips of historians. But strictly speaking, this kind of literary reading is not completely liberated from the historical context of the text. For example, even in a structuralist reading certain understanding about history is presupposed when it comes to certain vocabulary. In a structural reading, "tomb" in Mark 16:1–8 can be understood better if we know more about the tomb or tomb-like experiences in the historical time of Mark or Jesus.

The advantage of literary reading is obvious. It enriches the readers' reading experience when they attend to the power of the text one way or another. However, the weak point is also obvious because this approach, sandwiched between the historical approach and the reader-oriented approach, has a tendency of deemphasizing historical matters or the historical limitedness of the text. So a difficult question is: "How can we legitimate our literary reading when it has clear tensions with certain historical claims?" For example, there are at least two different possibilities of the meaning of Jesus: the one constructed from historical critical approaches and the other portrayed in the Gospels. I think there should be a fundamental gap between what happened in the past and what we understand about him through the writings after him. I think either of these two positions cannot annul the other possibility of meaning of Jesus because the text (as scripture) has roles to play (the "role" of the text).[17] However, if he or she merely assumes that Jesus portrayed in the Gospels (although each portrayal of the Gospels is different) is the same as the Jesus of history (although there is no singular construction of the historical Jesus), that is a great misunderstanding about Jesus and the Gospels as well, because as we saw, the texts (Gospels) are not interested in recording "history" about Jesus but in remembering the historical, theological significance of Jesus. On the other

---

16. For structural criticism, see Patte, "Structural Criticism," 183–200. For narrative criticism, see Rhoads and Michie, *Mark as Story*, 35–62. See also Gunn, "Narrative Criticism," 201–29.

17. Schneiders, *The Revelatory Text*, 11–25.

hand, if he or she insists that the four portrayals of Jesus in the Gospels are wrong because the historical Jesus is not correctly reflected there, this is also clear evidence of arrogance, because the Gospels have functions in historical communities. Namely, the portrait of Jesus in the Gospels makes sense and becomes truthful for the readers of the Gospels, as Hans Frei observes that the identity of Jesus and his presence go together.[18] That is, who Jesus is cannot be separated from what he shares in the narrative of the Gospels.

Reader-Oriented Approach: "Meaning in-front-of the Text"

Because of this weakness, a third approach to the text emerges: the reader-oriented approach. Reader-response criticism, poststructuralist, feminist, and postcolonial readings are part of this hermeneutical enterprise, in which the reader (ideal or real) takes the center stage in interpreting the texts. Though complex, this reader-oriented approach takes the question of the reader seriously and asks: Who is this reader that reads the text? In soft reader-response criticism, the reader is understood mainly as the implied reader of the text, which is different from the real reader.[19] For example, Stanley Fish, in his early career, advocated a natural flow of the text (passive role of the reader). But in his later career, he changed to a free flow of reading the text (very subjective reading).[20] However, Wolfgang Iser mediates between the passive role and the active role of the reader. Both the text and the reader are important to meaning making. A text has its own intrinsic flow or theme that the reader should follow. Yet the text does not provide the reader with everything he or she needs to understand. In other words, there is a gap or lacuna that the reader has to fill in because of a lack of clarity in a flow of the text. The reader's role is to fill in this gap by reading back and forth, because otherwise the texts are not clear enough for the readers' understanding.[21]

18. See Frei, *The Identity of Jesus Christ,* 12–45.

19. McKnight, "Reader-response Criticism," 230–52. See also Vanhoozer "The Reader in New Testament Interpretation," 301–28.

20. Fish, *Is There a Text in This Class?*

21. Iser, *The Act of Reading.*

Ideological-Critical Approach: "Meaning as Construction"[22]

But the reader-oriented approach that I am concerned with does not stop here. The notion of the reader is more far-reaching than reader-response criticism in general would suggest.[23] The scope of the reader includes flesh-and-blood readers in a variety of life contexts, in a variety of disciplines.[24] For instance, feminist and postcolonial readers problematize both the text and readings of others by pointing out both the imperial ideology encoded in the text and the imperialistic readings of others.[25] These real readers take seriously not only who wrote the text but also who interprets it and for what reason. For example, various levels of human ideology are examined in the text and others' readings. These real readers, from a variety of life contexts, use all kinds of textual methods (historical or literary) to critically study the text, and expose the oppressive voice in the text. The meaning of the text here is viewed as the "reader's critical construction." For example, some feminist readers read Pauline texts of women's degradation from a historical critical mindset and reach the conclusion that women's degradation or subordination is wrong, regardless of Paul's position or intention on the issue. For instance, 1 Cor 14:33–36 tells of a situation in which women in the church at Corinth are being oppressed. This oppression is understood as wrong because God is supposed to stand with these oppressed. Feminist readers also use literary criticisms such as narrative or rhetorical criticism or ideological criticism, through which they reveal dominating ideologies in the text or in other interpreters. For example, Lot's wife has been read traditionally as an example of disobedience to the command of God, which results in becoming a pillar of salt. But some feminist readers read this story

22. Segovia, *Decolonizing Biblical Studies*, 3–52.

23. Beardslee, "Poststructuralist Criticism," 253–67.

24. See Clark-Soles, *Engaging the Word*, 127–48. We see the diversity of publications in this area of a diverse reading of the Bible. For example, Patte, ed., *Global Bible Commentary*; Brenner, Lee, and Yee, eds., *Genesis*; Blount, Felder, Martin, and Powery, eds., *True to Our Native Land*; Bailey, Liew, and Segovia, eds., *They Were All Together in One Place?*; Guest, Goss, West, and Bohache, eds., *The Queer Bible Commentary*; Felder, ed., *Stony the Road We Trod*; and Adamo, ed., *Biblical Interpretation in African Perspective*; Liew, *What is Asian American Biblical Hermeneutics?*

25. Fewell, "Reading the Bible Ideologically," 268–82. See also Segovia, "Reading the Bible Ideologically," 283–306. See also Schneiders, *Written That You May Believe*, 127. See also Lancaster, *Women and the Authority of Scripture*. Regarding a postcolonial approach to the Bible, see Segovia and Sugirtharajah, *Postcolonial Commentaries on the New Testament Writings*; Dube, *Postcolonial Feminist Interpretation of the Bible*.

very differently; for example, Lot's wife (unnamed) is a model of caring for the community she left behind.[26] Or symbolically, she becomes seasoning salt that prevents the decay of the community.

Poststructuralist Approach: "Meaning as Deconstruction"[27]

In addition to this feminist or postcolonial approach, the so-called post-structuralist reading (mostly in a deconstruction reading) further challenges the traditional reading habits of finding the normative voice in the text.[28] In this reading, the reader is deconstructed along with the text because not only is the real reader unstable or interests-driven, but also, the text itself is not fixed in the way that it involves intertextuality. In a sense, there is no clear dividing line between the text and the reader. A text is not a given on its own as if it had some kind of ontological or permanent power affecting readers everywhere. Derrida critiques logocentrism and a singular construction of meaning that fails to account for multiple contexts and an interaction of signifiers.[29] Meaning is not a given in the text but is negotiated as he says: interpretation is "a knot of negotiation" full of "different rhythms, different forces, different differential vibrations of time and rhythm."[30] Meaning is "technical and representative" as Derrida continues:

> All signifiers, and first and foremost the written signifier, are derivative with regard to what would wed the voice indissolubly to the mind or to the thought of the signified sense, indeed to the thing itself. . . . The written signifier is always technical and representative. It has no constitutive meaning . . . This notion remains therefore within the heritage of that logocentrism which is also a phonocentrism: absolute proximity of voice and being, of voice and the meaning of being, of voice and ideality of meaning.[31]

26. Gunn, "Narrative Criticism," 201–29. See also Akhmatova "Lot's Wife." See also Jeansonne, "The Daughters of Lot."

27. The term "de(re)construction" means an ongoing deconstruction and reconstruction of any text and meaning. See Kim, *Christ's Body in Corinth*, 104n14.

28. Derrida, "Différance," in *Deconstruction and Context.*

29. Derrida, "Différance," in *Margins of Philosophy.* See also his interview, "The Villanova Roundtable."

30. Derrida, *Negotiations*, 29.

31. Derrida, *Of Grammatology*, 9. Derrida also states ". . .one is always working in the mobility between several positions, stations, places, between which a shuttle is needed" (Derrida, *Negotiations,* 12).

Therefore, rejecting a singular notion of the body and the text,[32] Derrida introduces a différance connoting two things: to defer or to differ. Meaning should not be taken as permanent and each meaning should be different in contexts. Derrida states that "différance is the name we might give to the 'active,' moving discord of different forces, and of differences of forces, that Nietzsche sets up against the entire system of metaphysical grammar, wherever this system governs culture, philosophy, and science."[33]

For Derrida, deconstruction is possible because the written text is not a correct or genuine mirror of reality. Therefore, the search for a fixed meaning is an illusion. Rather, meaning, in its most faithful form that allows for a self-critical, humbling spirit, is a negotiation between readers, signifiers and contexts.[34] Derrida does not believe in one, fixed, universal meaning in any written text.[35] This critique is twofold. One is to deconstruct the text. Another is to revolutionize the concept of text, the boundary of the text, which includes written and unwritten texts such as cultural location. Not only is the written text deconstructed but its readers as well. The best term to account for his meaning search can be found in the neologism "différance."[36] Hermeneutically, it is possible to pursue multiple, complex meanings without claiming to have a single, universal truth/knowledge about the body.[37] More importantly, deconstruction itself is not a method but a spirit or meta-critique of logo-centrism.[38] In the end, deconstruction itself is not a purpose; Derrida's ultimate interests lie in the vision for a just world, and the reconstruction of such a world based on more diversified views and contexts.[39] Likewise, the meaning of the text here is viewed as "de(re)construction" in the sense that any reading is constantly deconstructed and reconstructed. A deconstruction approach is suspicious about both the text and the reader, not because there is no meaning in the text but because there is a tendency of absolutism or fundamentalism by the readers. The emphasis of Derrida's deconstruction, which is not a method but an attitude toward the text, does not simply claim that that there is no

---

32. Derrida, "Différance," in *Margins of Philosophy*.

33. Ibid., 18. See also Derrida, "The Villanova Roundtable," 12–15.

34. Derrida, *Negotiations*, 29.

35. Ibid.

36. Derrida, "Différance," in *Margins of Philosophy*.

37. Derrida, "The Villanova Roundtable," 12–15.

38. Ibid., 9.

39. Ibid., 12–15.

single meaning of the text but that there should be no single dominating voice in the text at the expense of all other voices or meanings of the text.[40] Derrida's approach is not to destroy meaning as such, but to deconstruct absolutism or fundamentalism that blocks human dignity, freedom, and equality.[41] In a deconstruction reading, the text is more than the written text, and involves many forms of text—the inter-text and life text in history and today. Derrida states: "What I call *text* is also that which 'practically' inscribes and overflows the limits of such a discourse. There is such a general text everywhere that this discourse and its order (essence, sense, truth, meaning, consciousness, ideality, etc.) are overflowed."[42] So it is hard to distinguish the text from the reader and vice versa because both of them are coterminous.[43] Among all the paths between texts and reader's contexts, it is the reader who ultimately constructs meaning—meaning in each time of reading.

Summary

We have explored the way of reading the Bible both as scripture and historical writings. Then we surveyed a variety of approaches to the text. We also found out that there are deep tensions between the historical-critical approach and the reader-oriented approach. Whereas the former emphasizes historical, particular meaning based in ancient life context, the latter highlights a reader-responsive reading in today's life context, often at the expense of historical meaning. In fact, some literary readings can be naïve if historical realities of the texts are ignored. Conversely, some historical readings can be arrogant if the role of the text as scripture is denied. In all of these discussions, the most important lesson is this: ultimately, the reader decides the meaning of the text. Of course this job is not performed solitarily but critically and faithfully in honor of the polyvocality of the texts. To know more about the reader, we now turn to the next chapter.

---

40. Derrida, "The Villanova Roundtable," 1–28. See also Kim, *Christ's Body in Corinth*, 5–9.

41. Derrida, "The Villanova Roundtable."

42. Derrida, 59. See also Barthes, "Theory of the Text," 31–49.

43. See Gadamer, *Truth and Method*, 345–447. See also Palmer, *Hermeneutics*, 194, and chapters 11–12. See also Risser, *Hermeneutics and the Voice of the Other*, 83–116.

Questions for Further Reflection

1. Think about the idea of text. Is it fixed or open?

2. What does the text refer to? Who is the author? Single or collective?

3. Is the Bible different from the other sacred books? In what ways? Is there similarity or difference?

4. How are individual texts authoritative or sacred? Who decides?

5. Are all the books of the Bible equally valid and important or selectively authoritative? Why?

6. List various ways of reading texts. Why are there many ways? Is the diversity of textual methods good or dangerous?

7. Evaluate the statement "texts do not mean, but we mean with texts."

CHAPTER THREE

Contextuality: *Why* Do We Read?

Contextuality involves all aspects of the reader (real or intended): living conditions (personal or social), life experiences and perspectives, hopes and despairs. Every reader has his or her issues or needs to be addressed. No one reads the text like a robot run by a program. Of course, this does not mean that the reader can manipulate the text to fit his or her own needs regardless of the historical context of the text.[1] In fact, context is a concept of fluidity on two levels. First, context concerns the real reader's circumstances, which are not fixed and therefore need to be interpreted. Since the reader's life context is so complex and diverse, sometimes he or she does not know all about the context. In this sense, self-knowledge or self-criticism may be crucial even before one reads the text. Self-knowledge is the mode of positive attitude toward oneself, claiming his or her agency in lives. Self-criticism, on the other hand, is the mode of negative attitude toward oneself, questioning what he or she knows. Therefore, when one analyzes his or her life context, these two modes of attitude must be considered. Second, context also concerns the historical context, which is also flu-

---

1. This book's basic approach to biblical interpretation is different from a traditional "exegetical" approach in which, as Krister Stendahl proposed, there are two kinds of meaning: what it meant then and what it means now. In this book, however, meaning of a text comes from both the text and the reader. In other words, contextuality permeates ancient texts and readers, ancient or modern. In this regard, all readings are contextual. For a traditional approach to biblical interpretation, see Fee, *New Testament Exegesis*, 1–38; 144–54. See also Stendahl, "The Bible as a Classic."

id and needs to be interpreted. Often we assume that the historical context is clear with a single dimension of text, but that is not true. Undoubtedly, the meaning of a text depends on how we reconstruct ancient contexts. Then why is this double meaning of context important in the business of interpretation? The simple reason can be that the real reader can communicate with ancient texts or ancient readers.

All in all, contextuality provides the reason for reading the Bible. The real reader must engage the text from all feasible perspectives, insofar as a mutual dialogue between the reader and the text holds true. Because of this nature of contextuality and the reader's engagement, the Bible can be read for many purposes in diverse contexts. In the following we will see a few reading contexts and purposes: individual and devotional reading, reading for guidance in social and political life, and reading in theological education. The goal of this chapter is to see the role of the reader and the purpose of reading. Furthermore, we have to ask ourselves whether all contextual readings are equally good. If not, what can we say about the role of the reader?

Individual and Devotional Reading

A first context for reading the Bible is individual and devotional reading. Indeed, for thousands of years countless persons, religious and non-religious, have read the Bible as a source of spiritual guidance and moral insight. This kind of individual reading is good, but a problem may arise if this individual reading of the Bible only stays within the personal realm (like those who say that the purpose of the Bible is individual salvation only, nothing more nor less) and has nothing to do with society as a whole.

Silence in one's social space is also a political action by inaction, one that shapes the fabric of society as a whole. Borrowing the idea of "opportunity cost" from the field of economics, we can say that each member of society involves an "opportunity cost"—it is the cost incurred when an individual passes up an opportunity to participate in the society at large. The idea is that when we do not live fully, involving the personal and the public space of our lives, the loss of opportunity, that is, its cost, could be enormous. A social opportunity cost involves the loss of social goods in various forms; it arises from an individual's missing an opportunity to participate in society.

This kind of directive implies that reading the Bible only for matters of personal salvation would entail great cost like an opportunity cost that occurs in society. This cost may be explained as follows. Jesus' saying of the rich not entering the kingdom of God cannot be understood merely in terms of charity or in one's spiritual attitude toward the poor. When the message of Jesus is reduced to an individual sphere of life, that is, a charity-giving sufficiency, the society is bitterly going through a bigger class gap between those who have and those who have not, because charity-based help for the poor does not help improve their situation but to aggravate as the economic system runs against them.

From an economic justice point, we can easily understand why Jesus says that harsh saying about the rich. That is, what is evil is the fact that the rich's savings account money can save millions of starving people who are unable to find adequate jobs. The kingdom of God that Jesus refers to is not a future kingdom of immortal souls but a kingdom of God's justice and peace here on earth. If some people are starved to death, there is no kingdom of God realized.

Likewise, Paul has a similar concern about the unfair living conditions where the poor suffer while others have more than they need. Thus Paul says: "It is a question of a fair balance between your present abundance and their need, so that their abundance may be for your need, in order that there may be a fair balance (*isotes*). As it is written, 'The one who had much did not have too much, and the one who had little did not have too little'" (2 Cor 8:13–15). Here the key word is the Greek word *isotes* (balance or equality) that needs special attention from the reader. Of course, Paul does not force his church members but invites them to act on the basis of volunteerism (2 Cor 9:6–14). Similarly, "as it is written, 'He scatters abroad, he gives to the poor; his righteousness endures for ever'" (2 Cor 9:9).

Reading for Guidance in Social and Political Life

A second context for reading the Bible is when it is read for guidance in matters of social and political life.[2] People often take to the streets, with the Bible in hand, to advocate their own social or theological agendas. Some for example are "pro-life," being anti-abortionists; others are "pro-choice," advocating the right of women to choose between having an abortion and

2. John Stott investigates a diversity of contemporary issues on the basis of biblical teaching. See *Decisive Issues Facing Christians Today,* 149–61.

giving birth. Both groups often resort to the Bible to defend their theological or social position. Scholars, however, are quick to note that the Bible is not crystal-clear about abortion.[3] There are divergent interpretations of the laws concerning abortion in the Hebrew Bible. Moreover, there is also a great chasm between biblical times and life today. Whichever position is taken, however, "pro" or "anti," there are consequences that follow; real people are affected. Our point here is that any participation in society based on the Bible, however important, involves a certain cost, good or bad.

When Christians read the Bible for guidance in their social and political life, they inevitably choose issues that evoke more of their attention than others. Whereas some people care more about personal issues such as abortion or homosexuality, others care more about issues of social justice. Christians tend to choose their social issues, depending on their personal convictions about the Bible. A few years ago, some fundamentalist Christians in Korea prayed that Buddhist shrines throughout the country should be destroyed. Some of them attempted to destroy the statue of the legendary founder of old Korea, called *Dangun,* because they believe that these temples and their statues are idols and therefore evil.[4] As we see here, no reading is neutral, but has consequences. So the point is that we should be mindful of the notion of love of God and neighbor.

Reading in Theological Education

Reading in theological education is certainly one of reading practices through which professionals are educated and nurtured. Scholars, theologians, pastors and other leaders read the Bible not only for teaching or leading people but for deepening their own understanding of the texts. In a recent study of the state of theological education in the United States, published in his book *Pedagogy of the Bible,*[5] Dale Martin discovered that most protestant seminaries teach the historical critical methods as the primary, fundamental approach to the Bible. The working principle of the historical critical method is that the meaning of a text resides in the historical events (persons, ideas, etc.) to which the text refers, and is therefore both distant and distinct from the life of the text's modern readers.[6]

3. Kim, "Lex Talionis in Exod 21:22–25."
4. Kim, "Christianity in South Korea," 696–97.
5. Martin, *Pedagogy of the Bible.*
6. Stendahl, "The Bible as a Classic."

According to Stendahl, the primary task of biblical interpretation is to establish what the text meant in its original setting. The application of the text to contemporary life can only be a secondary task—one derived only after the original meaning of the text has been ascertained.[7] The value of the historical critical approach is evident in the sense that a text certainly refers to specific ideas or events. So in its normative sense the historical critical method understands texts on their accuracy in representing events, persons, ideas, etc. external to the text itself. Stendahl believes against emergent postmodernism and the current hermeneutical discussion, that what a text meant and what it means are two different things, that one could know objectively what the text had meant in its original setting, leading then to its subjective appropriation (or dismissal) by the reader.

But the point we are making here is that this is not the only way of reading the Bible. In my view, a better way of reading the Bible is to read a text both as an object and a subject by way of the reader's critical and faithful engagement with the text. As Dale Martin suggests, theological education should return to the premodern or postcritical reading of the Bible in which the text and the reader are not separated from each other but are engaged together.[8] Martin advocates what he calls the "theological interpretation of scripture," which he distinguishes from merely studying a text in pursuit of its historical information.

The point here is that "meaning" is always subjective; meaning does not inhere in texts but arises from interaction with texts. Martin emphasizes that the ultimate purpose of studying the Bible is not merely about the past but understanding the religious experience of early Christians in their lives. This shift of emphasis from the past to the present is significant because the role of scripture is recovered in theological education. Martin's point is timely so that we might teach and practice the Bible differently, beyond the traditional, historical approach to the text. Daniel Patte also treats the Bible in this way, and his earlier semiotic studies have been transformed into a more constructive, ethical interpretation of scripture. He emphasizes the reader's choices in the process of interpretation.[9]

7. This kind of traditional exegesis or biblical interpretation is explained in Michael Brown's little handbook *What They Don't Tell You*. Brown helps seminary students to survive under this traditional scholarship environment.

8. Martin, *Pedagogy of the Bible*, 1–45.

9. Daniel Patte is a pioneer in the study of contextual biblical interpretation. I owe him much of my thought and insight in this study. Patte names three elements of interpretation: contextual/relation choices, theological/hermeneutical choices, and analytical/

In reality, however, exegesis is still considered different from interpretation. Most students and scholars consider biblical exegesis to be a historical search for meaning, informed by the original context of the text. This kind of historical approach is not wrong in itself, but the point being made here is that it is not the only way of reading a text. [10] In fact, exegesis means interpretation and involves various possibilities of meaning, depending on various textual approaches and theory of interpretation.[11] What is needed is not simply to learn or teach specific methods or skills of exegesis as such but to learn or teach theory of interpretation so that we might be liberated from the captivity of an "original meaning complex."[12]

This complex occurs because the learned society or scholars tend to impose on others the privilege of scholarship based on historical meaning, as if it were the only correct approach to the text. This assumption is especially true and real for clergy persons, who have gone through intensive seminary education. Mark Powell has engaged in an experimental study of this problem. He asked clergy persons to read Lk 3:3–17 (the story of John the Baptist) and answer the question "What does this story mean?" Most of them write something about the original meaning of text in a certain way.[13] For example, one clergy person states: "Luke knows the Parousia has been delayed, and he writes to people who may be troubled by this. Here he wants to emphasize that the judgment of God will come eventually, even if it seems to have been delayed. This judgment will establish justice on all the earth."[14] Only when they are asked the question "What does this story mean *to you*?" do they begin to write something that begins to create an intersection between the text and their own lives. For these pastors, there

textual choices. Slightly modifying his terminology, I name them, respectively: readers, theological lens and text for this book's purpose in exploring the criteria for solid interpretation. See Grenholm, Cristina and Patte, "Overture."

10. Books about the traditional exegesis (historical or literary) are necessary but not all about biblical interpretation. These books include Fee, *New Testament Exegesis*; and Barton, *The Nature of Biblical Criticism*.

11. Now it is widely accepted that meaning is understood diversely, depending on theory of interpretation. See Segovia, *Decolonizing Biblical Studies*, 3–50.

12. I use "original meaning complex" in the sense that students and scholars are preoccupied with the historical search for meaning, without engaging the text from their perspectives.

13. Powell, *Chasing the Eastern Star*, 28–56.

14. Ibid., 43.

is a tendency to develop a two-step structure of meaning between what the text meant and what it means today.

By contrast, laypersons answer the same question ("What does this story mean?") very differently. One layperson states: "When I read this story I am inspired by the portrait of what a biblical preacher really can be. John the Baptist proclaims the word in a way that deals with the everyday stuff of people's lives—how to serve God wherever you are, be it as a tax collector or as a soldier. . . . This is the type of witness I would like to be."[15] Powell's conclusion is that laypersons do not tend to distinguish between the text then and the text now. The point here is not that there is no original meaning or that the historical approach to the text is wrong. The historical approach is necessary and has value. But the point is that the historical approach is one among many methods.

In fact, even the historical critical approach can be misused or mistaken, as John Dominic Crossan explains.[16] According to him, when researchers search for meaning in history, there are two kinds of difficulty involved: *an impossible delusion and a possible illusion.*[17] He defines them as follows: "The possible illusion is narcissism. You think you are seeing the past or the other when all you see is your own reflected present. . . . The impossible delusion is positivism. It imagines that you can know the past without any interference from our own personal and social situation as knower. Positivism is the delusion that we can see the water without our own face being mirrored in it."[18]

Although Crossan points out difficulties in the historical search for Jesus, we also find similar difficulties in our historical studies of the texts. We need to ask the following questions when we search for meaning in history: "What is history? Whose story or history is reflected? Who tells the story and whose voices are left out? Therefore, ultimately, the historian's job is not to describe what is what, but what is why, which means he or she should take positions. There is nothing in a text that can be explained by historians or theologians as value-neutral.[19] From the flip side, while this limitedness or contextuality of the reader cannot be avoided, it can be brought into the text, not in the way that any reading goes, but in the way that the reader

---

15. Ibid., 46.
16. Crossan, *The Birth of Christianity*, 41.
17. Ibid.
18. Ibid.
19. Tracy, "Interpretation of the Bible."

engages the text in terms of his or her life experience. Especially in a reader-driven textual approach we are advocating here, the reader's life context is not a negative element to the interpretation but a positive element because it is equally read with the text. Namely, the reader's life context can help the reader to see certain aspects of the text very well, and vice versa.

Summary

We have explored the meaning of contextuality that applies to the text and the reader as well. We also saw how important it is to recognize the different contexts and purposes of reading the Bible. An individual devotional reading is important to the growth of one's personal faith journey. But even this personal reading could benefit from a critical reading of the texts as done in seminary contexts. Moreover, this devotional reading could take social issues seriously. With these interactions and intersections with other ways of reading, the experience of a personal reading would be deeper, richer than before. Likewise, the reading for guidance in matters of social and political life also has a purpose, and the experience of reading can be deeper by interacting with the personal reading. The last context of reading the Bible is a professional educational setting where the Bible is studied through critical faithful inquiries without easily being absorbed into a particular doctrinal reading. Even this theological education can benefit from a personal and public reading of the text. As we see here, particular contexts or purposes of reading also must be checked with each other because context is fluid.

Questions for Further Reflection

1. What is the concept of context or contextuality? Is it limited to the reader or to the text?

2. Why is there diversity of life contexts in which people read the Bible?

3. Are ancient readers of the texts also contextual? Here ancient readers refer to the members of the religious community for whom particular texts are produced or read.

4. Is it possible that modern readers can communicate with ancient readers? What is the condition for such a communication and what does it mean to communicate in this context?

5. Why is the contextuality of modern readers important in interpreting texts? Is a contextual reading an eisegesis in the sense that it is a willy-nilly reading? What is the condition to avoid an eisegesis?

6. Does a text address all life contexts that we may need to be resolved?

7. What is the particular role of the reader when he or she engages the text?

Chapter Four

Engagement: *What* Do We Read?

In this chapter we will incorporate the previous discussions about textuality and contextuality into a coherent paradigm of engagement that
I call "the process of critical contextual biblical interpretation." Actually,
textuality and contextuality are not fixed; they are also objects of interpretation or engagement. But in this chapter what I mean by engagement is a
heuristic term that emphasizes the reader's role in terms of how one de-
termines a final meaning. To see how the reader makes a final decision, we
have to understand the process of contextual interpretation in a systematic
fashion. It begins when the world of the text (textuality) meets the world
of the reader (contextuality), as Hans-Georg Gadamer refers to a melting
of horizons: a horizon of the text and a horizon of the reader. He criticizes
historicists who view the meaning of the text as conceptual knowledge only
and emphasizes dialectical hermeneutics in that understanding is participation with the text. Likewise, Richard Palmer observes as follows: "Over
against the myth of purely conceptual and verifiable knowing, Gadamer
places his carefully enunciated historical and dialectical concept of 'experience,' where knowing is not simply a stream of perceptions but a happen-
ing, an event, and encounter."[1]

As we see here, every act of interpretation is a dialogue between the
reader and the text; therefore, we cannot avoid the contextuality of the
text and of the reader. Because of this contextuality, any reading of the text
involves a process/space of engagement, summed up with this following

---

1. See Gadamer, *Truth and Method*, 345–447. See Palmer, *Hermeneutics*, 194, and
chapters 11–12. See also Risser, *Hermeneutics and the Voice of the Other*, 83–116.

statement: "We are reading the Bible." In it, the three elements of interpretation (see *Table 1* below) are identified: "we" (the reader), "are reading" (the theological lens), and "the Bible" (the text). The most important operational decision is "what to read"—a theological lens, like a camera lens, that focuses on particular aspects of theology or a particular view of the text. *What to read* is like the steering gear of a ship, whose operation is determined by the ship's primary goal at the moment and the environment of the sea. The former is comparable to contextuality of the reader ("why to read"), and the latter to the entity of the very text ("how to read"). Like a voyage, reading the text involves the text (the sea), the reader (the ship), and the theological lens (the steering gear). These elements are interdependent with one another and work together. We will see in detail below how this three-element-interpretation works.

Table 1

WE	Are READING	THE BIBLE
The reader	The theological lens	The text
Contextual/relational choice	Theological/hermeneutical choice	Analytical/textual choice
Why do we read?	*What do we read?*	*How de we read?*

The first element "we" consists of actual readers of the Bible who read from various social locations and in diverse life contexts.[2] Daniel Patte calls this element "contextual/relational choices" because it involves the reader's choices concerning his or her life context. The central questions here are: Why do we read? Who are we as readers? We readers often forget whom we are when reading texts.

The second element "reading" has to do with the theological lens employed in interpretation, which can be explained through a different concept of theological vocabulary or view of the text. Patte calls this element "theological/hermeneutical choices" because it involves the reader's choices concerning the theological view of the text. Here the main questions are: What do we read? What kind of theological key to reading this text is needed? What is the role of the text? An analogy of picture taking will be helpful to understanding this element of "what to read." When we take a picture in a forest, we have to decide which object to shoot, the zoom ratio, the viewing angle, the shooting distance, the exposure time, the shutter speed, and so forth. Reading the text is similar to taking a picture. The

2. Segovia, ed. *Reading from This Place* Vol. 1–2.

reader decides which character, theme, or theological concept to focus on.[3] For instance, when we read a passage of Jesus' crucifixion, we will have to choose and articulate which concept of crucifixion (or atonement) is in view in the text. Often the text in question involves more than one concept of atonement (penal substitution theory, satisfaction theory, ransom theory, and moral sacrifice theory, and so forth). See the *Excursus on Jesus' Death in Context* on page 68.

The last element "the Bible" is the written text. Patte calls this element "textual/analytical choices" because it involves the reader's choices concerning textual methods. The main question here is: How do we read? To answer this question, as we saw in the previous chapter, we have to grapple with questions such as, "What is the Bible? Or what is a text?" The Bible is both a historical and theological product, and it plays a role of scripture for people throughout history.[4] Before even deciding what to read, the reader has to wonder about the living, dynamic quality of written texts that can change or challenge his or her view of the text.

As these three elements of interpretation indicate, the process of interpretation is vibrant and complex. We want the Bible to be read and taught in its full capacity as sacred scripture rather than merely as an ancient literature of the past. We want the Bible to be read critically and faithfully in the recognition of both the divine and human elements in it. We also want the Bible to be read as a source of human transformation, as it contains multitudes of diverse human religious experiences. In the following we will see in detail more about the theological lens and the role of the reader in the process of interpretation.

The Theological Lens

In a frame of "we are reading the Bible," "are reading" has to do with the theological lens of the text. That is the question of what do we read. This part of "reading" has to do with a viewing angle among many choices of theological interpretation. The adjective "theological" needs explanation, since there are many different aspects of theology. First, the word "theological" is understood in terms of the multiple concepts of theology. For example, when we read the accounts of Jesus' crucifixion in the Gospels or

3. Patte, *The Challenge of Discipleship*, 43–63. See also Patte, *The Gospel of Matthew*, 15–42.

4. Morgan, *Between Text and Community*, 1–29.

of Paul's interpretation, the meaning of the cross is variegated. Satisfaction theory says that Jesus' death satisfies God's demand of justice. Ransom theory says that Jesus' death is a ransom price for releasing the captives from the devil. Penal substitution theory says that Jesus' death is a substitutionary punishment instead of sinners. Moral sacrifice theory says that Jesus' death is a challenge to his followers so that they might follow his example of sacrifice. There are more than these views regarding the meaning of Jesus' death. So when we read the accounts of Jesus' crucifixion, we should decide which theological concept we are drawing and why we do so. In fact, all of these theological concepts have tensions with one another. At one level, it is important to recognize many different theological concepts at work in the process of interpretation. At the same time when one focuses on a specific concept or theme, the overall interpretation should be consistent in view of his or her context, textual approach and the role of text. In the next chapter we shall come back to this topic when we talk about the issue of what constitutes the criteria for good biblical interpretation.

Second, the term "theological" also has to do with the different roles of the text. Daniel Patte, for example, applies different metaphors for the different roles of the text. The metaphors he suggests are: "lamp-unto-my-feet, corrective glasses, canon, family album, empowering word, etc."[5] All these metaphors serve to explain the role of the text as it addresses various contextual problems: "lack of knowledge, wrong knowledge, lack of will, lack of faith/vision, lack of ability, etc."

Let us see how these metaphors work in relation to contextual problems. For example, Davies and Allison interpret Matthew 28:16–20 with an implicit concern for discipleship based on true power and knowledge of Jesus (Davies and Allison, 676–91). The role of the text is that of the canon, in the sense that disciples should do what Jesus commanded them to. On the other hand, Elaine Wainwright reads the same text through the different roles of the text: corrective glasses and empowering word (Wainwright, 114–18). Corrective glasses, as a metaphor through which we see discipleship more clearly, are possible by comparing women disciples and male disciples. As for her, the first witnesses of Jesus' resurrection are disciples, who boldly go and tell good news to the downcast male disciples after their betrayal of Jesus. From Wainwright's perspective, these women are disciples who help recover the male disciples. Only after the intervention of the women do the male disciples encounter the risen Lord with a feeling of regret and doubt about Jesus. When they come back to Jesus, they

---

5. Patte, *The Challenge of Discipleship*, 60–63.

are eventually restored to their place as disciples and are commissioned. Through this metaphor of corrective glasses, we see the meaning of discipleship differently as it is told by Matt 28:16–20. The other metaphor of "empowering word" has to do with empowering women in this text so that they might live the life of discipleship without hesitation.

The Reader

In a frame of "we are reading the Bible," "we" corresponds to the final element of interpretation, the reader. Actually, the reader is involved everywhere in the process of interpretation, as we saw before. There is no interpretation without a reader/hearer. It is the reader who decides textual methods and the role of the text in terms of why it is read. But the scope of the reader is not limited to the flesh-and-blood reader of today. There are the diverse readers behind writings in historical communities and the diverse readers/interpreters throughout history. If we look at this vast arena of readers in history and in texts, we realize that all of them are real readers in their times. In oral cultures, people tell and hear stories, interpreting them in their life contexts, and retell their stories to the next generations. Now these next generations inherit these retold traditions or stories, reinterpret them in their life contexts, and again retell them to the next generations. This process repeats itself in history and is indeed cross-cultural. People in history are never the same. In oral culture, there was also another kind of real reader who lived differently from the multitudes in society. We should remember that there are many divergent authors/readers in ancient times, writing and rewriting, interpreting traditions in their time and context, reinterpreting the received traditions in a new context.

A typical example of divergent voices (therefore divergent real readers in ancient times) in the tradition is to be found in the documentary hypothesis (J, E, D, P), which suggests that the four distinct voices/traditions are interwoven in the fabric of the Torah.[6] The eighth century BCE prophets such as Micah or Amos represent another kind of real readers. At every crucial moment of ancient Jewish history such as the exile in Babylon, and the Jewish Revolts there have always been real readers, who not only rewrite the previous stories to make better sense in their living contexts but act accordingly.

---

6. For more about the formation of the Pentateuch, see Coogan, *The Old Testament*, 47–56.

Jesus, Paul, church fathers and many people in history are real readers too in their times. Real readers of our day are different from implied
readers in the text. So now we, as real readers, engage these ancient readers
(both elites and low class). We, as real readers, can learn from the experience of all of these readers of texts and in history. Yet there might also be
something that we should not follow. So the task of interpretation is ever-
going to people throughout history. It is crucial to discern what is good
and acceptable to God and neighbor when we read the text in view of this
vast array of readers both behind the texts and in historical communities in
front of the texts. To critically, faithfully engage the ancient real readers, we
have to know *who we are* as real readers. Only then can our dialogue with
the text be fruitful and helpful to our lives today. That is why I think it is
a scandal when contemporary readers read biblical texts without knowing
their own history and life contexts.

The Role of the Real Reader

With this important task of critical and faithful interpretation, it is worth
talking about particular implications about the role of the real reader. First,
the real reader does not follow texts as if they were waiting to be excavated.
They are also historical participants in the world of interpretation through
conversing with various others in the text and in other readings. As there
are numerous historical participants in the Old and New Testaments, there
are also numerous readers in our time who read the Bible and reinterpret it
in their life context. So it is legitimate or necessary for us as real readers to
respond not only to the Bible but also to various readers in history and today.
This view of the participatory reader is possible because God is not known
only through the Bible. God is known through us too, and vice versa. It is like
saying that God is the God of Moses, the God of the living God, and the God
of "me." As Abraham departed Ur on his journey of faith because of his sense
of calling from God, we also depart our journey of faith for an unknown
future. In this regard, the role of the real reader is very important because
the real reader should discern God's unfolding work in the Bible and in the
world today, because, in fact, there is no single view of God in the Bible nor
a single view of theology in the world. Ultimately, it is the task of the reader
who converses with the past, the present and the future.[7]

---

7. Soulen, *Sacred Scripture*, 171–90.

Second, the real reader also has to recognize that he or she is a very limited human being. In our classroom for example, we can look at a complex picture such as *Picture 1* below and ask students: "what do you see?" Obviously, students' answers will vary: a chalice in the middle, an old man playing the guitar, a woman standing at the gate, or an old couple facing each other, and so forth. Then we would ask again: Which is the correct view? They will realize that there is more than one meaning or interpretation of the picture. While the picture itself contains various meaning possibilities due to multiple small pictures in a larger picture frame, they cannot see all of these small sub-pictures at the same time. This realization by students is a time of sensing their limitations, humility, and solidarity with each other in a classroom. If one cannot see all at the same time, he or she should be ready to hear from others. Or, he or she should wait and try again later to see something more, or to see the whole picture clearer than before. One more analogy of climbing a mountain will be helpful. Imagine that a few people climb a mountain at the same time. What they individually see might be different. Even a few days later they will see still the very different things with each other. All these differences can be paralleled with the experience of reading a text. So we have to acknowledge that we are individually different, limited in our ability, and perspectival in our view of the world and the text.

Picture 1: An Old Couple[8]

8. Http://www.moillusions.com/2007/04/old-couple-young-couple-illusion.html. Web accessed on January 20, 2011.

The Real Reader and Politico-theological Questions

The real reader in our day also engages the real world as a whole and expands his or her interpretive gamut to a variety of issues in it.[9] Real readers today live in the world where theology and politics are interwoven with each other, and intertwined with so many other things in the world. For instance, ecology and its relationship to theology is a new concern today as well. From a perspective of political theology, nobody can escape living with neighbors or enemies. In America today there are so many different people living together. So the real reader should respond to the existence of neighbors. Who am *I* that respond to God's call? Ultimately, the political theological question boils down to: "What is an ideal relation between the self, one's neighbor and God?"[10]

In fact, the Bible contains stories of political theology that deal with the relations between self, neighbor and God. We variously practice political theology influenced by the readings of the Bible. For some, the neighbor is the object of mission, as they understand the Great Commission in such a way that they disavow geographical and cultural borders. In this view, removing the enemy is the main goal of political theology, with no sense of engagement with the difficult enemy. A typical case of this kind in recent politics is found in the Bush doctrine of the "preemptive strike." Some people might find their image of God from the warrior God in the Hebrew Bible. So they read the God of Israel as the one who commands Israelites to destroy enemies in Canaan. The idea behind it is that purity cannot be

---

9. In this book "political theology" is referred to as the works of scholars such as Žižek, Santner, and Reinhard, *The Neighbor*. The use of "psychotheology" in this book is derived from Eric Santner's book, *On the Psychotheology of Everyday Life*. For a variety of contemporary issues facing Christians today, see Stott, *Decisive Issues Facing Christians Today*.

10. Regarding our attitude toward others, a phenomenalist, Emmanuel Lévinas, helps us to understand the importance of the Other in our lives, as he observes: "To speak, at the same time as knowing the Other, is making oneself known to him. The other is not known, he is greeted. He is not only named, but also invoked" (Lévinas, *Difficult Freedom*, 7). See also Lévinas, *Alterity and Transcendence*, 29. Similarly, Julia Kristeva emphasizes "foreignness" in ourselves, as she observes: "By recognizing this strangeness intrinsic to each of us, we have more opportunities to tolerate the foreignness of others. And subsequently more opportunities to try to create less monolithic, more polyphonic communities" (Kristeva, *Revolt, She Said*, 63–64). I further argue that this strangeness may lead to a process of human transformation, as I wrote elsewhere. See Kim, "The Story of Hannah."

contaminated with the profane or that enemies are not the subject of conversation but the object of destruction.

This kind of ideology of removal is also found in the episode of Hagar's expulsion (Gen 21). Hagar and Ishmael are expelled because of Sarah's preemptive strike due to the fact that she did not like living together with them: "Cast out this slave woman with her son; for the son of this slave woman shall not inherit along with my son Isaac" (Gen 21:10). Even though the narrative of Genesis 16–20 supports Abraham's casting out of Hagar and Ishmael, based on Sarah's request, it is Sarah's jealousy or selfish mind that causes such a merciless expulsion by putting their life in jeopardy in the desert. On the other hand, we find the other side of the story, as God blesses Ishmael, moments later in the desert. God hears Hagar crying for life or death. The blessing of God is that Ishmael will become the father of many nations. Whereas some people might read this act of God as a mere sympathy to this poor mother and child without changing the view of a merciless God who executes the request of Sarah in narrative, other people can read this blessing of God to Hagar not as a mere expression of care but as a sign of reaffirmation that Hagar and Ishmael are also the same family of Abraham, or at least the family of God. In fact, Ishmael is Abraham's offspring (Gen 21:13), and it is Sarah who asked Abraham to sleep with Hagar to bear him a child. It is her decision to make Hagar a wife of him because of her impatience with the yet-to-be-born child, an heir of promise. From this alternative perspective that I propose here, Sarah's blunt, merciless request is a bad thing even at the face value of Hagar's haughty attitude toward her (Gen 16:1–16).

As we see here, we, as real readers, inevitably ask political theological questions: How can we account for this painful story in view of three subjects involved: self, neighbor, and God? Does God simply blindly support Abraham and Sarah even though they act unjustly? I actually heard a sermon at a local church: "It is God who intends Hagar and Ishmael to be expelled. It is God's plan." This sermon suggests that Hagar and Ishmael should follow God's command and will. But from a critical perspective, it is Sarah's problem that caused the expulsion of Hagar and Ishmael. It is not God who designed such a plan. Sarah and Abraham are weak and unstable even with God's blessings and promises. From a political, theological perspective, we can identify their limited vision in several ways: a narrow ideology of family and lineage, a narrow conception of community, and a narrow vision of God's family. Abraham and Sarah failed to do justice due to their dull sense of who they are in relation to Hagar and Ishmael. This failure could be stated as a failure of dealing with neighbor. Moreover, a more significant failure is that they forget who God is: God is the one who calls, promises, and saves people through faith. But in this episode Abraham and Sarah do not live up to God's grace and mercy and treat Hagar and Ishmael as "others"—the object of control or expulsion. What they do not understand is that God loves Hagar and Ishmael too, as we know from that fact that God blesses them in the desert.

Also, a great misunderstanding for them is to think that they can love God without loving their neighbor. Actually, their difficult time with Hagar and Ishmael could be a moment of transformation in terms of finding their own humanity before God and neighbor. Times of stress due to the existence of Hagar and Ishmael can be moments of new hope and solidarity, affirming that Hagar and Ishmael are also the same family of God. The expulsion of Hagar and Ishmael is not the precondition for God's blessings for Abraham and Sarah. They actually got what they want: the child of promise, Isaac. As we glimpse here, if we approach this story from a political theological perspective where three subjects are involved, the meaning of this text is deeper than the usual reading that privileges Abraham and Sarah. Therefore, if we, as the real readers, are keenly aware of this kind of political theological issue that I showed here, our reading would be healthier than otherwise.[11] If we extend our thinking or perspective to psychotheological aspects of self, our interpretation will be richer still.

Summary

In this chapter we have explored what the art of interpretation means and how the three elements of interpretation are linked together. We also saw the need of a critical yet faithful (theological) interpretation. While affirming the diversity of human life and interpretation, we should also check the irresponsible or unclear readings of the Bible. Ultimately, this leads to the need of criteria for solid interpretation to which we now turn.

11. Kim, "The Story of Hannah."

Questions for Further Reflection

1. What is engagement of the text and the reader? Is it possible to interpret the text without engaging? What difference is there between an engaged reading and disengaged reading?

2. Think about the three elements of biblical interpretation: the reader, theological lens, and the text. Does this three-element-interpretation make sense? Why or why not?

3. Talk about the needs of the reader. Explain the relation between the reader's needs and the text's role. Does the text address all issues of the reader?

4. What is a theological lens? How do theological concepts of vocabulary affect the reader? Also, talk about the role of text.

5. Think about atonement as you read the idea of "Christ died for us" in Rom 5:8, Gal 1:4, 1 Thess 5:6–10, and Mark 10:45. How many concepts of atonement are possible? Which view of atonement is the better one? Why?

6. What is the role of the reader in deciding the right interpretation?

Chapter Five

Criteria for Solid Interpretation

While different groups of people or religious traditions can forge their own criteria, be they critical or pre-critical, doctrinal or liberating, the different sets of criteria must be evaluated because not all criteria are helpful or solid.[1] This is where I start to explore the discussion about criteria for solid interpretation.[2] Since criterion derives from the Greek verb *krino* (to judge), we have to judge which interpretation is solid or better than the other. This means that one has to explain why his or her interpretation is legitimate and healthy in a certain context. As I wrote elsewhere, what we need is not a naïve imagination but a critical imagination, which "can be explained by the following illustration. Suppose that a person wants to fly like a bird, which is a good and necessary imagination, and so jumps off from the mountaintop in an attempt to fly. That person will be killed because of his or her naïve imagination. But if a person devises a flying

---

1. For example, Catholic tradition emphasizes "the three criteria for reading the Bible," according to Vatican II: 1) "Be attentive to the content and unity of the whole Scripture"; 2) "Read the Scripture within the living tradition of the whole Church"; 3) "Be attentive to the analogy of faith." See the site: http://www.mariedenazareth.com/432.0.html?L=1 Accessed Date: Nov. 25, 2011. For fundamentalist groups one criterion is literalism or inerrancy of the scripture. For most Protestants, one criterion will be "justification by faith." For liberation theologians, the message of God who liberates people in oppression will be an important criterion. While all of these criteria are legitimate within their own contexts, they are not equally helpful to contemporary society. How can we talk about these criteria? On what basis can we judge which is better than the other? To answer these, this chapter provides a set of rules or decision basis.

2. Because of this accountability, ethics of biblical interpretation is important, as scholars already registered their concerns. See Patte, *Ethics of Biblical Interpretation*, 1–36. See also Schüssler Fiorenza, *Rhetoric and Ethic*, 1–56.

machine, then he or she can fly; this exemplifies that a critical mindset and creative imagination should work together."[3] Therefore, any ideologies or criteria should be evaluated or challenged.

Actually, the need of the criteria for solid interpretation arises because of the complex process of interpretation that involves the three elements: the reader, the text, and the theological lens. A vast array of interpretation is possible, but not all readings are equally sound or healthy. Indeed, some readings are poorly conceived or argued, and there is no strong textual evidence to such a reading. At times, the reader tends to absolutize his or her reading at the expense of other readings. In fact, as we saw *Picture 1*, our eyes cannot focus all objects in the picture at once. Therefore, on one hand, we choose to focus on some things in the picture. On the other hand, our limited perspectives or abilities in interpretation can be a stirring moment of humble and authentic encounter with the mystery of God.[4] The mystery is, according to Paul, that we do not have full wisdom or knowledge (Rom 11:33). Ironically, because of this human limitedness, we can honor the mystery of differing contexts in our lives and also struggle to understand the deeper meaning or implication of our lives.[5] With this kind of attitude toward our weakness or limitedness in interpretation, we can interpret the text. That is, in order to appreciate the whole picture of the text, we will have to try to see it from the bird's eye-point of view by looking at big and small things together, and back and forth. This back-and-forth reading can be compared to the relation between the forest and trees, as Schleiermacher suggests the hermeneutical circle.[6] In order to understand the forest well, we observe the trees in a close look and move back and see the whole forest from a distance.

Given the complexities of interpretation, the important task is how to explore the criteria for solid interpretation or how to tell which

3. Kim, *A Theological Introduction to Paul's Letters*, 5.

4. Because of this limitation, each interpretation at any given moment should be deconstructed at another moment. For instance, the "kingdom of God" (*basileia tou theou*) in the Gospels can be understood as a heavenly realm, which is good for a person who needs to overcome the burdens of current life by imagining a better future in heaven. Otherwise, beyond or outside of this specific need, this reading would be naïve because "the kingdom of God" can be understood as "God's realm" on earth here and now. Even the same person may read the kingdom of God differently at different times.

5. Phyllis Trible rightly observes: "The concept of authority includes power to receive and give multiple meanings in its diverse and changing contexts" (Trible, "Authority of the Bible," 2248–60).

6. Schleiermacher, *Schleiermacher: Hermeneutics and Criticism*, 231–35.

interpretation is good. Furthermore, who can decide? While the different theological traditions may claim different set of criteria, there is a need of establishing good criteria so that we may need to test the effect of interpretation. As human dignity is a basic moral value in a modern democratic society, universally applicable to all people, we need criteria for solid interpretation. The universal vision or criteria that I am talking about differs from that of the Empire where some are privileged at the expense of others. When we use the language of "universal" here, it associates with "the basic value morality" that focuses on human dignity and welfare, or the "universalizing faith" with which people live for others without worries.[7] As initial explorations about such criteria, I will suggest the following three criteria for the sound biblical interpretation.

The First Criterion: Critical Diversity and Solidarity

The first criterion for solid interpretation is critical diversity and solidarity. We will examine three parts in this section: What is diversity? What does "critical" mean? What is solidarity? First, diversity should not be understood as "anything-goes."[8] Actually, differences between cultures, for example, are not recognized as different until they are exposed to other people in another culture who are different from them. When this exposure or encounter takes place, there is tension or conflict with other people because they are different. In this cultural encounter, true diversity may be possible, not by maintaining cultural or ideological boundaries but by engaging the differences of others.[9] This kind of image of diversity also applies to biblical

7. There are four different types of morality: taboo morality, allegiance morality, the morality of universal laws, and basic value morality. Taboo morality has to do with the ego-centered behavior. Allegiance morality has to do with group loyalty. People behave to belong to a group. The morality of universal laws emphasizes universal laws that affect all human beings. In contrast, the basic value morality emphasizes the well-being of all people. See Barnes, *In the Presence of Mystery*, 153–80. Interestingly, this morality corresponds to the "universalizing faith" in James Fowler's stages of faith. Fowler lists six stages of faith: "Intuitive-Projective Faith, Mythic-Literal Faith, Synthetic-Conventional Faith, Individuative-Reflective Faith, Conjunctive Faith, and Universalizing Faith" (Fowler, *Stages of Faith*, 117–210).

8. Kim, *Christ's Body in Corinth*, 97–102.

9. The notion of diversity is re-appreciated in biblical interpretation. For example, the episode of the tower of Babel in Gen 11:1–9 is interpreted very differently than the traditional one in which the primary cause of sin is arrogance of humanity toward God. In other words, in a traditional interpretation, scattering of people by God (as a result,

interpretation. Namely, the diversity of biblical interpretation is not war-ranted just because there is diversity. There must be an ongoing process of a critical dialogue between the text and the reader, and between the readers across the border, including all kinds of readers in history.

On the other hand, diversity is not an ornament or a supplementary thing to unity or to the status quo of institutions or society. When cut flowers are put in a vase and placed on the dining table at a feast, they look good and pleasing to guests around the table. But from the perspec-tive of flowers, it is not a pleasant thing because they are cut off from the soil—their native land. They look beautiful but their beauty soon fades away for there is no life in them. The moment that they are cut off, they are removed from their life support. This analogy of cut flowers teaches us that diversity is not a thing of superficiality when some are happy at the expense of others. True diversity means living together with equality and mutual care. Likewise, this analogy also suggests that solidarity must be part of community building.

Second, "critical" is a term that points to an attitude or approach that characterizes a "deep and wide" search for meaning of the text. The con-notation of "deep" refers to a deep understanding of historical reality and thus of context of the text. When there is a voice of oppression, Jesus' death challenges those who overpower the weak. A "deep" reading is made pos-sible when the reader challenges the current practices of reading focused on individual salvation. It also helps to reconstruct the history and people in the text with a view of justice and to recover the neglected voices of the text. A "deep" approach to the text looks at the past in a new or different way—through the eyes of Jesus' death that reflects all spheres of human life. Paul's experience of pain and suffering in his ministry can be understood differently (more deeply) than before if we compare his understanding of pain and suffering with that of the Stoics. The Stoics generally avoid talking about pain (*lype*) or suffering perhaps because they want to avoid the topic altogether. Perhaps they are scared to talk about the crucifixion of slaves, and therefore do not need to develop a counter-word for this *lype* (pain or suffering). It is an irony that they develop different words in response to various modes of human emotion: joy (*chara*) in place of pleasure (*hedone*),

---

speaking in different languages in different places) is considered God's punishment. But in a new interpretation, the human problem in this episode is people's gathering in one place (i.e., not scattering is a problem), wherein they do not worship God but trust their power, living in one place (speaking one language). So God scattered them to live in diversity. See Hiebert, "The Tower of Babel."

volition (*boulesis*) in place of desire (*epithumia*), and caution (*eulabeia*) in place of fear (*phobos*).[10] But there is silence about pain (*lype*). Why do the Stoics not find an alternative solution word for pain or suffering?[11] Perhaps they do not know what to do with it or want to be silent forever by avoiding difficult issues.

However, in a deep search for the meaning of pain and suffering in Paul's texts, we understand a deep side of Paul's theology of the cross. This kind of deep search is possible because the reader critically re-imagines realities or conditions of life.[12] Whereas for the Stoics and others the cross of Christ does not make sense because it is a scandal to Jew and foolishness to the Greek, for Paul with new imagination it becomes a crucial event and a way of life (like virtue) in the face of death-like situations where slaves are exploited, tortured, and killed if they rebel against society. Christ's death symbolizes both God's love (solidarity) for the oppressed and God's judgment for those oppressors. Christ died in the midst of bringing God's love and justice to people in need. God's love is to remove pain and suffering, and Christ showed God's love, confronting the evil of pain and suffering, inflicted by the powerful and elites in society. This sacrifice and love of Christ is a comfort to those who are weak and oppressed, because they know through this cross God loves them. So it is a message of hope and solidarity for these people. More than that, this cross also exhorts members of the community to live in solidarity with others in similar situations. On the other hand, Jesus' death means God's judgments on those who do not live up to love, sacrifice, and solidarity shown by Jesus. Jesus' death is a radical truth for the world when there is

10. Pereboom "Stoic Psychotherapy."

11. Welborn, "Paul and Pain." See also Welborn, *An End to Enmity*, 380–481.

12. As I wrote elsewhere, the role of critical imagination is important in biblical interpretation: "We will need a critical imagination that engages both history and theology seriously in Paul's texts and contexts. The use of critical imagination can be explained by the following illustration. Suppose that a person wants to fly like a bird, which is a good and necessary imagination, and so jumps off from the mountaintop in an attempt to fly. That person will be killed because of his or her naïve imagination. But if a person devises a flying machine, then he or she can fly; this exemplifies that a critical mindset and creative imagination should work together" (Kim, *A Theological Introduction to Paul's Letters*, 5). Similarly, Amos Wilder cautiously emphasizes the role of imagination: "Imagination is a necessary component of all profound knowing and celebration; all remembering, realizing, and anticipating; all faith, hope, and love. When imagination fails doctrines becomes ossified, witness and proclamation wooden, doxologies and litanies empty, consolations hollow, and ethics legalistic . . . Then that which once gave life begins to lull and finally to suffocate us" (Wilder, *Theopoetic*, 2).

no justice and love. Jesus' death speaks God's wisdom that shames those who are powerful and that chooses "what is foolish in the world to shame the wise; God chose what is weak in the world to shame the strong" (1 Cor 1:27).

So a "deep" approach to the text helps the reader to look at the world differently. Likewise, "wide" is not separated from deep; it is like two sides of the coin, because "deep" requires a wider look at human life reflected in the text and in the world. Paul's interpretation of pain and suffering as shown above is a good case in that we see both "deep and wide" aspects of pain and suffering that transforms the world focused on God's love and justice. In this way Paul seems to respond to the Roman world where pain and suffering is not properly dealt with. That is what his gospel can provide those who are powerless and hopeless. As we see here, "critical" needs a deep and wide approach to the text and the world. Thus "critical diversity" must mean that diversity is to be engaged in critical contexts of life and the world through checks and balances. Critical diversity tests "all things" in our interpretation: all the diverse peoples, diverse voices, diverse methods, and the unknown mystery. Because of the nature of critical diversity, which includes all biblical interpreters across the borders, and across the disciplines, critical diversity should engage all these. Biblical interpretation is neither separated from other fields nor fragmented in its own little comfort zone.

Third, solidarity is to be a goal of critical diversity in interpretation. Here I prefer solidarity to unity because the latter involves a negative history of interpretation that unity is often understood as subsuming all differences, likely to be seen in the idea of the melting pot theory or assimilation into sameness. Solidarity emphasizes equality and mutual care. As we saw in Sarah's exclusive ideology, if we examine this episode from the perspective of solidarity, the expulsion of Hagar and Ishmael is wrong and immoral.

The Second Criterion: Congruence of Interpretation

The second criterion for good biblical interpretation is congruence between the three elements of interpretation (the reader, theological lens and the text). All these three elements should cohere with one another. That is to say, there should be a correlation among the human condition, the root cause of that condition, one's view of scripture, and the teaching of the text (see *Table 2* below).

Table 2

Human condition	Root cause	View of scripture	Example of teaching
Depression, low self-esteem	Lack of faith/ trust in God	Loving parents (family album)	You are the beloved child of God.
Confused, wayward	Lack of knowledge	Lamp-to-my-feet	You should know the truth.
Arrogance	Lack of will	Canon	You should accept others.
Egoistic	Crooked vision	Corrective glasses	You are because of others.
Victims	Lack of ability	Empowering word	You can do it!

The human condition and the root cause are derived from the reader's life context, but, as is so often the case, the reader may not be well aware of his or her life context, whether personal or communal. *Knowing who we are as readers* cannot be emphasized enough. The more we know about our life context today, the more we will faithfully engage the text. View of scripture is the role of the text in providing solutions to the human condition or root cause. Let me illustrate what this means. If we read Luke 15:11–32 (the story of the two sons), our resulting interpretation will be very different depending on the human need. In the case of "depression or low self-esteem" as a problem of the reader, the root cause of the problem can be a lack of faith in God. Then, the needed scriptural support or image can be "loving parents" ("family album"). The teaching of the text is "you are a loving child of God." The father's steadfast love and care is emphasized, as the father waits for the son day and night. In the case of "wayward" life as a main problem, the root cause may be a lack of will to live in family. The younger brother's purposeless life can be looked at seriously. So the teaching of the text may have to do with providing correct knowledge and motivation with which he can stay in the family. In the case of "arrogance" as a problem, attention will be given to the older brother who lacks the will to accept his brother. In the case of "egoistic attitude" of the younger brother, attention will be given to his crooked vision of community or family. Through a miserable life, he realizes that family is the most important and returns to the father. Even though he is responsible for all this misery, he is determined to seek the father's help.[13]

13. Even in preaching if we read (preach) the same passage always in the same way and insist that true meaning of the texts remains the same, it is evidence of bad interpretation because there is more than one meaning of the text. Likewise, if we always preach

As we see above, all these different readings are plausible or valid in each context because differing contexts of the reader allow them to engage the text differently. If someone reads this text (15:11–32) with the same focus all the time, he or she ignores the power of the text (because the text addresses many things) and the diverse human conditions that demand multiple solutions. Likewise, if someone insists that there should be only one universal meaning of the text without considering these three elements of interpretation, danger ensues. Meaning should be understood as a critical dialogue between the text, the reader, and theological lens—a process that never stops insofar as the reader engages in interpretation.[14] So we need to make explicit our contextual/relational, hermeneutical/theological, and analytical/textual choices about the text. In that way we can contribute to an ongoing process of God's work in this world.[15]

The Third Criterion: Balance of Interpretation

The last criterion for solid interpretation is balance of interpretation by which I mean that solid interpretation engages the holistic aspects of life in the text. For this task, we have to use all methods of biblical studies. Among other things, political theology and psychotheology shed new light on our understanding of holism when we read the texts. In fact, the Bible is full of political theological stories in which we find three subjects of political theology: self, neighbor and God. For instance, in the Hebrew Bible we might ask this kind of political theological question: "How can we understand the role of God in relation to Israel and its neighbors?" So we, as real readers, ask: What are ideal relations between self, neighbor and God? The Bible is also read from the perspective of psychotheology, as I have written previously.[16] Here the question is: How do difficult moments of our life help our transformation? Balance is important in our

---

different passages of the Bible through the same theological lens, it is also evidence of bad interpretation. For instance, if we preach a sermon based on a theme of the love of God, and say that "God loves you no matter what" for whichever texts are chosen, without talking about the nature of the love of God in various life contexts, it would be a naïve sermon. In a situation of arrogance for example, the love of God should also include judgment of God, as a coin has two sides.

14. Schneiders, *The Revelatory Text*, 157.

15. Patte, *The Challenge of Discipleship*, 48. See also Patte, *Ethics of Biblical Interpretation*, 27.

16. Kim, "The Story of Hannah."

human life and biblical interpretation because we were meant to live in balance when God created us. With this kind of balance in mind, we will explore the idea of "balanced interpretation." First, it involves three modes of human existence: autonomy (individual life), relationality (community life), and heteronomy (religious life). The mode of autonomy concerns self-determination (rule by self) and emphasizes individuality based on strong self-consciousness. More or less, Western culture tends to emphasize this mode of life. The assumption is that if persons do the right things (autonomous human being), society as a whole would be right. In contrast, the mode of relationality emphasizes the web of human life, and the primary meaning of life is obtained through relationships with others. The mode of heteronomy is "rule by others." This mode of life easily accepts mysterious dimensions of life, including the experience of others and God. Interestingly, these three modes of human existence correspond with three elements of interpretation because, in my view, interpretation of the text involves the interpretation of human life through the text. For example, people who primarily see the world and human life through autonomy will read and interpret the text with a focus on individual, autonomous issues. The *Table 3* below shows corresponding relations between the primary mode of human existence and view of scripture, root cause, and relevant teaching of the text.

Table 3

Primary mode of human existence	View of scripture	Root cause of the problem	Relevant teaching in view of human existence
Autonomy	Canon	A Lack of knowledge or will	"I should do"
Autonomy	Lamp-to-my-feet	A lack of knowledge or will	"I will be informed"
Relationality	Family Album	A lack of vision or faith	"We are children of God"
Relationality	Corrective Glasses	A lack of vision	"I change my vision"
Heteronomy	Empowering Word	Powerlessness	"I need God's help"
Heteronomy	Holy Bible	A lack of faith or vision	"I am open to God"

As seen from the above table, the mode of autonomy is seen in the upper two rows. "Canon" and "lamp-to-my-feet" tend to emphasize an autonomous level of human existence, and the addressed human issue is to know God's will without giving much attention to others within or outside of the community. The root problem in this view can be a lack of knowledge or will. In this view of scripture, moral view is deontological in the sense that the issue is over whether we do things right. The mode of relationality is seen in "family album" and "corrective glasses" through which a bigger community for all is emphasized. So relationality is the primary concern in this view: how to live with others. The root problem would be a lack of vision or faith. In this view, moral view is perfectionist in the sense that a moral issue has to do with the embracing of the holistic community. The mode of heteronomy is seen in "holy bible" in which people are struck by sudden revelation of truth. This mode allows the reader to respect "others" as others, accepting awe-inspiring experience or insight from the text. The root problem in this case would be a lack of vision or faith.

Well so far so good. Each mode of human existence is necessary in our life but it does not represent the complexities of human lives. Put differently, each of these interpretations might not be the best if it does not address or show the balanced human life in the text, which means balancing these three modes of human existence. Therefore, while each of these interpretations in *Table 3* is plausible and/or valid in each context, each may not be the best if there is no balance in view of these three modes. Let us see how this works. A case of balanced interpretation is found in the story of Hannah (1 Sam 1:1–2:11), as I wrote elsewhere.[17] While the story of Hannah may be read from many different perspectives, the balanced interpretation addresses all modes of human life (autonomy, relationality and heteronomy). Hannah is an individual (self), who lives under certain social, political, religious conditions (relationality). Yet she goes through this difficult time of nothingness and is transformed through new faith in God (heteronomy). In the midst of storms of life due to her barrenness, Hannah should deal with neighbor and God, because, on the one hand, her childlessness is a stigma from the perspective of society, and on the other hand, it is also a problem of theodicy: "Why did God close her womb?" As we see here, one of the issues faced by Hannah is how to relate to these subjects (neighbor or enemy and God). Hannah's neighbors include Elkanah, her husband, Peninnah, another wife of her husband, the priest Eli and others in the community. If we read Hannah through a perspective of the holistic human life (based on three modes of human existence), we are not only helped by the text so that we might live such a life but we are also challenged by the potentials of the balanced approach so that we might be invested deeply in our otherwise torpid interpretation.

Likewise, balanced interpretation also involves three subjects of political theology: self, neighbor and God. How to articulate the relationships between these three subjects is closely related to how to configure three modes of human existence. Namely, self corresponds to autonomy; neighbor, to relationality; and God, to heteronomy. In fact, these three subjects of political theology fill the Bible: for instance, Israel's story can be read through that lens. Moreover, the early Church's story (or Paul's story) can be read similarly through that lens of political theology that involves the relationships between self, neighbor and God. Among other things, when it comes to interpretation of love in these three subjects of political theology, *three loves* (the love of self, the love of neighbor and the love of God) should be understood correctly and used as a relevant analytical tool of our interpretation of the text. So Kenneth Reinhard rightly observes about three loves:

> Love of myself is imaginary, the spectacular reflection on myself that constitutes the narcissistic ego in the mirror stage; and love of the neighbor is real, insofar as the neighbor harbors the strange kernel of enjoyment Freud and Lacan call the Thing. However,

17. Ibid.

this twoness cannot be reached directly and does not subsist on its own, Lacan argues, except by passing by way of the third love, never superseded, the love of God, which is the model of symbolic love, the love of the father that sustains the symbolic order. Hence, love of the neighbor includes within it the love of God, and together they constitute the Borromean knot of political theology. . . . The subject loves the neighbor only by means of the love of God, and loves God only by means of the love of the neighbor.[18]

Solid interpretation involves these *three loves* in balance. Let me illustrate. The recent Korean movie *Secret Sunshine* deals with this issue of *three loves*. In the movie a young mother struggles after her son was kidnapped and killed by a man in the neighborhood. Soon she is evangelized through a local church's persistent message that "God loves you." Eventually, she makes up her mind to forgive the murderer of her son and visits him in a prison. Facing the murderer, she breaks silence and barely begins a few words, and surprisingly, even before she gives a formal word of forgiveness to him, he joins her and proudly says: "I also believe in God, and God forgave me; I am very peaceful now." Suddenly, her face is hardened, confused, and angry with God. She thinks that she has to offer a word of forgiveness to him. The point of her anger is how he can bypass her in his relationship with God. This movie raises the issue of God's love in the face of a friend-enemy relationship. This issue is how one can love God without recovering a relationship with his or her friend or enemy.

Summary

In this chapter we have explored the three criteria for good biblical interpretation. All of these criteria are built on the three elements of interpretation (the text, the theological lens and the reader). I do not mean that this set of criteria is enough or fixed. I only hope that this discussion of criteria for good biblical interpretation will stimulate researchers and pastors, Christians and non-Christians, to rethink about the role of the Bible and its significance in their contemporary lives. In particular, I hope that this discussion will help seminary students to engage the Bible both critically and faithfully. In this way, I envision that the Bible as scripture continues to be read, evaluated, and appreciated in a variety of life contexts today, not because it is perfect in any sense or a perfect resource for all matters of

18. Reinhard, "Toward a Political Theology of the Neighbor," 71–73.

human life but because it includes tons of human religious experiences to which we also have to respond from a variety of perspectives. That is what Jewish and Christian traditions share. For example, Moses speaks to the next generation of people in the wilderness, and later Israelites in exilic time period reinterpret the early Jewish tradition in light of their new life context of Babylonian exile. Early Christians diversely responded to the preaching and teaching of the Jesus tradition, forming diverse communities and producing corresponding gospel stories rooted in both the historical ministry of Jesus and their life contexts. Therefore, there is nothing wrong with contemporary readers who respond faithfully to the Bible in their various new life contexts. Indeed, God is not the God of the dead but of the living. Therefore, the reader's context or role is crucial to our interpretation.

Questions for Further Reflection

1. What is bad interpretation? What are some symptoms of it? Be specific and take an example from your experience.

2. Why are bad interpretations not checked? What motivation is behind them?

3. What do you think the best criteria for biblical interpretation will be? List all of them and compare with others.

4. Discuss the suggested criteria for solid interpretation in this chapter: critical diversity and solidarity, congruence, and balance.

5. Interpret John 14:1–21 and develop your own set of criteria for solid interpretation. Explain them to others. This topic may be a group project.

Chapter Six

The Kingdom of God as a Test Case

"The kingdom of God" (*basileia theou*) frequently appears in the New Testament, especially in the Synoptic Gospels. Yet the meaning of it is not monolithic among gospels because the gospel communities interpret it differently in their life contexts. More complexly, the "kingdom of God" also appears in the Hebrew Scriptures, and we have to ponder its relation to the New Testament. In all of this, the crucial question is which concept of the kingdom of God we can find in each occurrence or in the Bible as a whole. This question involves the reader's choice and engagement with the text.

Since the critical contextual interpretation involves a particular reader, what is presented in this chapter is my critical, contextual reading of "the kingdom of God." All analysis and perspectives are mine. I am not proposing my reading is the best. I can only invite other readers to read with me. Like Derrida's notion of différance, each reading or meaning of the text should be different in other contexts and it should be deferred until later times, because clarity of meaning may come later.[1] I do my job, analyzing the text, evaluating interpretation results, and putting my theological reading on the table. Certainly, I read the text (the kingdom of God) with my theological lens, in the very context of life that I consider the most important today. For this goal, this chapter has three parts: the role of the reader, the analysis of the text, and engaging the kingdom of God. The primary questions about the reader are as follows: What issues are we faced with in contemporary society? What are particular concerns or issues in regards to the message of the "kingdom of God"? Then, we will examine "the kingdom of God" in the

1. Derrida, "Différance," in *Deconstruction and Context.*

New Testament and Hebrew Scriptures from a variety of perspectives. After this, we will see a possible mapping of critical interpretation. Lastly, we will compare all interpretations by criteria for solid interpretation and suggest the best interpretation given the life context today.

Human Existence and Creation Story

We, as readers, have to ask who we are in the world when we interpret the kingdom of God because the reader makes interpretation.[2] Furthermore, the notion of the kingdom of God requires some sort of the reader's position toward human existence in the world. To help us understand who we are or how we are made, let us take a look at two creation accounts in Gen 1–2. In the first account (Gen 1:1—2:4a), God creates male and female in the image and likeness of the divine (Gen 1:27). It seems that humans are created perfectly without physical vulnerability. The implication is that humans before the fall could live forever without death. The negative human experiences in the world are considered the result of sin (punishment).

But in the second account of creation (Gen 2:4–25) the Lord God forms *Adam* from the dust of the ground (*Adamah* in Hebrew) and breathes in his nostrils the breath of life (Gen 2:7). As a result, Adam becomes a living being (*nefesh*). The implication here is that Adam's weakness or mortality is natural, as the dust often stands for limitedness or weakness in the Hebrew Bible (Gen 2:7; 3:19; Eccl 12:7). From the two versions of creation, we know that we are made imperfect, weak, and limited. Even in the first account of creation, it seems that God did not create a perfect human being, because if "perfect" means a sinless human, human beings, logically speaking, should not have sinned. The question is why we are made with the double nature of humanity: a loft human being (image of God) and a dust-like human being (from the ground). As we see in the second account of creation, the first human (*Adam*) is formed from the dust.

2. Actually, the issue of "who we are in the world" is a crucial theological enterprise for me, as I teach and research biblical literature. My teaching philosophy is as follows: "I teach to engage in the knowledge of who we are in this world where we see one another as diverse. Diversity is not taken for granted but utilized as a source of critical engagement with others. I value both a critical and self-critical stance toward any claim of knowledge, truth, and reality and emphasize the following as pedagogical goals: learning from others, challenging one another, affirming who we are, and working for common humanity through differences. All in all, the goal of my teaching is to foster critical diversity and imagination in their learning process" (Kim "Teaching the Bible in a Different Culture").

Existentially speaking, the lesson is that we recognize limitedness or weakness in our lives as a necessary difficult element to human growth or perfection. Moreover, with this lesson we human beings may be awakened to the need for solidarity with other people because all are embedded in various forms of brokenness or weakness in our lives. Because we are not perfect, we need God and others. This kind of anthropological understanding about human existence may be vital to our interpretation, as we are engaged with the interpretation of the kingdom of God.

Some Critical Issues Today

There are a few important issues facing the church and Christians today. First, the issue has to do with the mission of the church. Often people think that the successful church is the one that has large membership along with many mission programs. But from a perspective of *yukjisaji* (meaning "to think from the other perspective"), this large church may be evidence of mission failure because, according to Jesus, people flock to an easy road. If the road of the church were difficult to take, perhaps not many people had joined it. Because this church provides an easy-to-accept gospel of prosperity, many people come to that church. A large church knows how to run the church on the basis of a successful marketing strategy, which satisfies the masses' needs. There is no need of discernment between what is right and what is wrong. Rather, there is a measure of success by which the reason for the church stands. There is no serious struggle in that church in terms of how to live with others. If the road is narrow and difficult to follow, not many people come to take it. Jesus says that whoever wants to follow him must bear his or her cross and abandon all the comforts and expectations of daily life. Thus we have to be suspicious of a larger church to see whether there is the gospel of the cross that looks beyond one's own life. Of course, we can hardly say that all the larger churches are unsuccessful, but the point is that we have to evaluate their mission results or programs from the perspective of *yukjisaji*.

On the other hand, we can say the small church is evidence of a successful ministry because what it involves a difficult path, a difficult gospel, which requires cost. The church is not popular and people hesitate to join. That is why the church is small. But the small church may be evidence of an unsuccessful mission too, when the mission is not well performed according to the model of Jesus. The point is that we have to judge the church, not by the appearance of the church but by the essence of the gospel practiced there.

Second, therefore, the issue has to do with the gospel that people understand and practice. In the synoptic gospels the centerpiece of Jesus' message (or good news) is the kingdom of God (*basileia theou*). But in contemporary religious lives most people understand this phrase mainly as a future kingdom of God, either immediately after death (soul entering heaven) or an eventual establishment of the kingdom of God on the last day. According to this view, the one who can enter heaven (as the kingdom of God) is the one who accepts Jesus as the savior who paid the price for God's justice for sinners (satisfaction theory of atonement) or who was punished instead of sinners (penal substitution theory). Or, the person is individually justified before God (individual justification once and for all). But the kingdom of God, as preached in the synoptic gospels, is not a heavenly place but a metaphor that points to the rule of God, characterized by justice and peace. Even the Gospel of John understands the eternal life as a metaphor that points to the presence of God or a quality of life with God, as we will see later. But for many, John's Gospel has been read through Platonic dualism in which the ultimate salvation is the soul's going into the heaven ("immortality of the soul").

Because of this kind of narrow understanding about the gospel, there are harmful implications to other people. For example, the problem is their judgmental spirit that denies others, other religions, cultures, or thoughts. The gospel is understood as a weapon by which other people or cultures are subsumed under the culture of Christendom. There is no strong urge of practicing the love of enemy or neighbors. They are looking to change others, never changing or challenging themselves. This is against Jesus' understanding of the gospel, as he summarizes the whole law and prophets with the double commands, based on Deut 6:5 and Lev 19:18. Similarly, Paul also says that love fulfills the law (Rom 13:8–10).

Third, the issue has to do with the otherworldly salvation and a dull sense of Christian ethics whereby God's justice in this world is sacrificed. Christian ethics becomes secondary because the world is viewed as transitory, not worth living fully or investing one's life fully. John Bunyan's novel *Pilgrim's Progress* is a good example that people buy this idea of a transitory world. This novel presents two kinds of problems. First, it has a tendency of promoting individualistic, pietistic faith at the expense of the community or the larger society.

Related to the first, second, there is no ethical drive toward reaching others with compassion or justice. A Christian's search for a heavenly home may be good, but his decision to leave his family seems problematic. It is hard for a person like me who has the culture of community to understand this Christian who leaves for his own heavenly home. This kind of storyline of the novel does not match the vision we see in biblical stories. Moses prays to God that the Israelites are saved from God's punishment (Exod 32: 31–32; Num 21:4–9). Abraham bargains with God to save the people of Sodom and Gomorrah (Gen 18:16–33). God sends Jesus as the Logos to give the life and light to the dark world (John 1:1–18). God did not send Jesus to take God's people out of the world. Jesus prays to the Father: "I am not asking you to take them out of the world but protect them from evil" (John 17:15). Jesus sends the disciples into the world. So the ministry of the Logos continues with the Advocate (*Paraclete*). Paul, like Moses, wants salvation of the whole people, Israel: "I could wish that I myself were accursed and cut off from Christ for the sake of my own people, my kindred according to the flesh" (Rom 9:3).

But in *Pilgrim's Progress* we do not see the other-centered spirit that looks beyond the self. In light of these scriptural witnesses, the Christian in the novel is not an ideal Christian that we are seeking. Perhaps the unnamed Lot's wife could be a better model to follow. She may have looked back at the city because of her nurturing concerns for the people behind her.[3] Regardless of whether she heard the command given to Lot ("do not look back"), the point is that, as feminist interpreters observe, she had concerns for the people behind. Actually, it is Lot who lingered in the city even after the angel's command that he must leave with his family. Perhaps, the command of "do not look back" was limited to Lot because of his lingering. Even if she had heard the command, her bold act of looking back to the burning city could be interpreted positively, because a pillar of salt means a sacrificial monument that next generations could remember her sacrifice or concerns for the city, or seasoning that blocks the decay of the city. Lot's wife may be a person deeply caring for the community and family.

Fourth, the issue also has to do with the atonement of Jesus. The idea of atonement is much more complex than we think. On the Day of Atonement (*Yom Kippur*), through symbolic holy sacrifices people (Israelites) are recovered to relationship with God (Lev 16; 23:26–32). The role of sacrifice

3. Gunn, "Narrative Criticism." See also Akhmatova, "Lot's Wife"; and Jeansonne, "The Daughters of Lot."

is reparation or mending of a relationship between them. A broken relationship needs some kind of sacrifice not merely because of individual sins but because of a broken covenant. The point of ritual is communal and reconciliation, not for satisfaction of God's justice because of individual sins. What are required on this Day of Atonement are not just animal sacrifices but a broken spirit and a contrite heart. Their relationship with God is restored because of the breaking of their hearts. The death of animals *per se* is not atoning. Their sins are covered not because of animal death but because of their repentance.

Likewise, Jesus' death as *hilasterion* (the mercy seat or atonement sacrifice in Rom 3:25) is not atoning because of his death. When people repent because of his death, they are recovered to God. Through Jesus' holy sacrifice showing God's love and justice, the believers are challenged to live like him. According to this view, Jesus died because other people did not die or did not want to die. In this view, it is not our faith but Christ's faith that manifests God's righteousness to the world (Rom 3:21–26). The believer's job is to have Christ's faith, which means participating in his life and death. That is what "in Christ" means in Paul's letters. In Paul's thought, faith is an action word, just as James put it rightly: "faith without action is dead" (Jam 2:26). There are lots of misunderstandings about Paul's understanding of faith. Paul quotes from Hab 2:4: "the righteous one shall live by faith." In the context of the Hebrew Bible, faith means trust, loyalty, and commitment. Thus it is natural for Paul to quote Hab 2:4 when he talks about faith in Romans 1:17. In Rom 2:13, Paul says that the doers of the law are the righteous ones. The faith Paul talks about is a genuine faith that seeks God's kingdom (or righteousness) for all people through the example of Christ.[4]

The Analysis of "The Kingdom of God"

Now with those concerns and issues about the kingdom of God that we discussed before, we, as real readers, enter the world of the text, "the kingdom of God." The texts have variant, diverse aspects of the kingdom of God. Therefore, it is important to study each text on its own, and in doing so we appreciate the distinctive voice of each and compare with other texts. In the following we will investigate the kingdom of God in the Hebrew Bible and the New Testament. What we attempt to do here is not a full-fledged reading of the kingdom of God in the Hebrew Bible and the New Testament.

4. Kim, *A Theological Introduction to Paul's Letters*, 64.

Rather, here our focus will be a survey of the kingdom of God articulated in ancient texts.

The Hebrew Bible

Since the majority of the Hebrew Bible reflects monarchical times after David, the kingdom language primarily refers to a political, human kingdom.[5] Before the Davidic monarchy in the tenth century BCE, Israel was made up of a loosely connected tribal union (confederacy) in which local chieftains ruled their own territory.[6] Shifting to monarchy, however, there were some tensions, as narrated in 1 Samuel, between those who wanted a strong king like other nations and those who supported a direct rule of Yahweh. In the narrative, Yahweh allows human kingship, and the monarchy becomes a political, ideological norm through which the Davidic kingdom is established. The Davidic house is the only anointed one with whom Yahweh makes an everlasting covenant (2 Sam 7; 1 Chron 17).

But this Davidic royal ideology and kingdom faces challenges because of the kingdom's division into two parts and also because of social crises caused by the elites' corruption and injustices. The eighth century BCE prophets like Amos and Micah harshly critique the injustices of society and the roles of the elite and the wealthy. Amos rejects their expectation of "the day of the Lord" and tells them that the day of the Lord would be the day of a doom (Amos 5:20). Jeremiah and Ezekiel also criticize Judean leadership at the brink of the Babylonian threat because the leadership moved away from the Mosaic covenant.

All these prophets are concerned with the restoration of Israel as an ideal state that worships Yahweh alone in Jerusalem.[7] They are critical of kingship but do not reject kingship itself because that is a reality. On the one hand, they yearn for a return to the Davidic, Abrahamic covenant, and on the other hand, they are envisioning a new kingdom of God that extends to the whole world. For this, Israel becomes a beacon or light to the nations

---

5. Birch and Brueggemann, et al., *A Theological Introduction to the Old Testament*, 215–56.

6. Coogan, *The Old Testament*, 223–29.

7. The so-called Deuteromistic theologians and prophets influenced by them, including the later priests such as Ezekiel, push to a return to the Mosaic covenant and to the worship of Yahweh at Jerusalem. After the Babylonian exile experience, strict monotheism appears. See Michael Coogan, *The Old Testament*, 409.

(Isa 42:6; 49:6; 60:3). Ezekiel draws a map of such an ideal state in the future and makes Yahweh the God of all people.

A few Psalms also emphasize God's kingdom that covers all people and the world. Psalm 103:19 reads: "The LORD has established his throne in the heavens, and his kingdom rules over all." Likewise, Psalm 145:11–13 reads: "They shall speak of the glory of your kingdom, and tell of your power, to make known to all people your mighty deeds, and the glorious splendor of your kingdom. Your kingdom is an everlasting kingdom, and your dominion endures throughout all generations. The LORD is faithful in all his words, and gracious in all his deeds." In the Book of Daniel as well, we also see a similar thought of God's sovereignty over the kings of mortals: "How great are his signs, how mighty his wonders! His kingdom is an everlasting kingdom, and his sovereignty is from generation to generation" (Dan 4:3).

In addition, in Dan 4:17: "The Most High is sovereign over the kingdom of mortals; he gives it to whom he will and sets over it the lowliest of human beings." Here we see an ideal vision of God's kingdom (*malkuth Yahweh*) that God is the center of the kingdom (1 Chr 28:5; Ps 22:28; 45:6; 66:7; 103:19; 145:11–13). In other words, God's kingdom is not a physical kingdom of Israel anymore but a rule of God for all people. The centerpiece of that vision has to do with an irenic setting of a future state where the wolf will live with the lamb (Isa 11:6). Of course, this ideal future will happen through Israel. But what is not clear throughout Jewish literature after Babylonian exile and during long time of personal and national turmoil (through empires of Babylon, Persia, Greece, and Rome) is who will be a right heir to continue this vision of an ideal state. A majority of Jews believe that a future deliverer of the Israelites is to be a descendant of David. Others believe that must be particular individuals such as prophets or priests. In sum, the idea of the kingdom of God (as God's kingdom) emerged when there had been personal, social, national crises in Israel. Prophets maintained a balance between criticism of the state and hope for the people. Overall, the kingdom of God is about God's sovereignty on earth as the prophetic writings illustrate.

The New Testament

The Historical Jesus

We do not have direct accounts about Jesus other than the later Gospels written around 70–90 CE, and the earliest written book in the New Testament is Paul's letter of 1 Thessalonians (around 50 CE).[8] Therefore, we have to depend on the early Christian writings to reconstruct the historical Jesus.[9] In doing so, we have to begin with preceding contexts of Jewish life in first century C.E Palestine. First of all, the Roman Empire and Hellenism are important backgrounds to understanding Jesus' message about the kingdom of God. Caesar's kingdom is gained through military might and economic exploitation. The Roman Empire is blessed and anointed by the Roman deity. Hellenism's ideal is one world with hierarchical unity at the center. In contrast, Jesus' proclamation of the kingdom of God seeks God's rule on earth. Second, local situations in Palestine should be linked with Jesus' message of the kingdom of God. Jerusalem leadership was corrupt, aligning with the Roman Empire. Various groups of Jews respond differently to total crises of their state. Pharisees emphasize a renewal for the law. Some people join the armed resistance group against Roman rule. Essenes withdraw to a desert and wait for God's radical intervention through the final battle between the children of light and the children of darkness. In socio-economic terms, lives of people were ruined; peasants and lower classes lose their livelihood because of high taxation and natural, social disasters caused by famine and the patronage system. All of these crises led to the first Jewish war in 66–70 CE.

With this kind of historical backgrounds in mind, the historical Jesus' preaching of the kingdom of God, as recorded in Mark and Luke, can be best understood as the reign of God; the center of his kingdom message is a counter-cultural, reforming movement.[10] As the prophet Jeremiah claimed a renewal of the heart at the brink of national disasters, Jesus asks people to

8. Regarding sources, problems, and methods of the historical Jesus, see Ehrman, *The New Testament*, 237–52. See also Holladay, *A Critical Introduction to the New Testament*, 58–99.

9. Regarding the historical Jesus debate, see Clark-Soles, *Engaging the Word*, 103–126. See also Keck, *Who is Jesus?* 1–150; Charlesworth and Weaver (eds.), *Jesus Two Thousand Years Later*, 1–117; and Keener, *The Historical Jesus of the Gospels*, 1–13.

10. Borg, *Jesus*, 23–189. Borg's study of the historical Jesus is very much in this direction. The historical Jesus is understood as a person filled with the Spirit, who challenges and transforms the society. See also Wink, *The Human Being*, 67–112.

return to God. Jeremiah prophesies that the Lord will make a new covenant with the house of Israel and the house of Judah, not because the old covenant is wrong but because they broke it (Jer 31:31–34). So the solution is that the Lord God will put his law in them and write it on their hearts. What this implies is that a new covenant is a matter of heart. Jesus inherits the prophetic tradition of a renewal message like Jeremiah. Jesus asks people to break their heart for God, the God of the covenant. In other words, Jesus' God is the God of love, as he summarizes the whole law and prophets with the double commands: the love of God and the love of the neighbor. The way Jesus preaches and acts on the kingdom of God is non-violent in nature but expressly active enough to show his resolve to change the world. He cleansed the temple with whips. He certainly knew that his preaching of God's kingdom would end up with his death. His cross is the price of justice. Read in this way, Jesus' preaching of the kingdom of God is not about the otherworldly future kingdom or some sort of a spiritual kingdom. Jesus is both a radical reformer based on the Jewish prophetic tradition and an apocalyptic prophet who yearned for a completion of God's kingdom in the future.

The Canonical Gospels

Now let us look at the synoptic Gospels and then the Fourth Gospel. Through these gospel stories, we are reading not the historical Jesus but the interpretation of early Christians beginning 70 CE. The primary meaning of these sources has to do with the particular gospel communities.[11] We can understand the historical, social, and religious issues faced by a particular community behind each gospel. While we appreciate the particular ministry contexts and contents of the gospel communities, we also have to compare them because of their divergent experiences in communities.

Overall, the kingdom of God (*basileia theou*) in the canonical Gospels does not refer to the immortality of soul. Rather, the kingdom of God can be either a metaphor of God's rule or a future kingdom of God on earth.[12] As we will see, even in John's Gospel, the kingdom of God is not a heavenly, spiritual thing apart from the earth here and now. Similarly, "the kingdom

---

11. Regarding historical and literary introduction to the Gospels, see Ehrman, *The New Testament*, 88–216.

12. Keener, *The Historical Jesus of the Gospels*, 196–213. See also Räisänen, *The Rise of Christian Beliefs*, 79–113.

of heaven" in Matthew's Gospel is not an otherworldly heavenly place that souls enter after death. In Matthew, the kingdom of heaven is interchangeable with the kingdom of God since for Jews God's name is too holy to be pronounced. With this caution and common understanding of the Gospels, we will investigate the kingdom language in each Gospel. As an overall introduction to the Gospels, see "Jesus' death in context" (excursus below).

Excursus: Jesus' Death in Context[13]

When approaching the thorny concept of atonement, we must consider the death of Jesus — the ultimate act of atonement — and what it means to our lives as Christians. This is not as simple or obvious as it may sound. In my observations, Protestant teaching and preaching most frequently tends to advance a single view of Jesus' death: The "penal substitution" theory. This position holds that "Jesus died, instead of me, because of my sin. Jesus was punished in my place. As a result, I am not punished, and I am saved once and for all."

Unfortunately, this position is often viewed as the only correct one, but it is also a very limiting one. When exploring the concept of atonement, it is risky to emphasize any one interpretation of Jesus' death, particularly the penal substitution theory, to the exclusion of others. This type of absolutism is over-simplified and may lead to exaggerations such as those seen in the extreme violence of the Mel Gibson film *The Passion of the Christ.*

Focusing on just one view of Jesus' death, particularly the "penal substitution theory, often causes us to ignore alternatives that may be more complex, realistic, and spiritual. For instance, the "moral sacrificial" theories that are discussed later in this article emphasize important cultural and ethical aspects of Jesus' death that call upon us to respond in mature, decisive ways.

I suggest, then, that any study of atonement must take into account the diversity of interpretations about the cause and meaning of the death of Jesus. Who was responsible for the execution of Jesus. . .and why? We must consider the social, political, and theological context in which Jesus' ministry and death occurred and the particular cultural context from which a specific interpretation about his death emerged.

---

13. This is my article "Jesus' Death in Context." Used by permission of *Living Pulpit.*

Each of the Four Gospels offers a distinct view of the death of Jesus, indicating that a multiplicity of interpretations existed even among early Christians. Each interpretation also tells us something about a particular community of believers. Modern Christians can find important lessons in all four views, but depending upon the particular time, place, and culture in which a contemporary Christian lives, one or the other of the gospel views may seem more applicable to daily living. The Gospel of Mark emphasizes that Jesus lived an "others centered" life in the midst of a self-centered society. His death then, for the salvation of others, is a call to the members of Mark's community to live a risk-taking life for the sake of others. To put it still another way, "giving his life for many" (Mk 10:45) becomes a moral lesson to the Markan community, showing them how to live selflessly and morally in a self-centered society that also threatens them with persecution. The Gospel of Luke advances the "innocent prophetic" interpretation of Jesus' death. The people of the Lukan community are exhorted to repent for their ignorance about the Messiah and for their "innocent" (without knowledge of his true identity) killing of him. In this context, as the people comprehend true repentance, they cannot help but recognize and acknowledge God's love for all. In the Gospel of Matthew, Jesus' death is viewed as the culmination of a life of integrity. . .a life that totally rejects every vestige of hypocrisy, even if this behavior leads to condemnation and death. John's Gospel presents Jesus' death as his achievement of glory, victory and eternal life, for all of us. An important issue for the Johannine community is to live the empowered life of the Spirit now, in the midst of hatred and alienation from the Jewish community. The message here is that life's "death-like" situations will turn to victory, not just in the afterlife, but here and now.

This multiplicity of interpretations is cause not for confusion but for celebration, because it offers us a holistic understanding of Jesus' death, an act of atonement that has been interpreted, preached, and lived out differently within the context of each faith community. Our preaching and teaching needs to recognize this diversity of traditions, diversity of interpretations, and diversity of human life, so that we can better serve in a diversity of contexts and offer space for others to enter in. Ironically, that space opens widest when we realize the aspect of Jesus' death that seems to rise above all cultural contexts — the radical message of inclusive love he had for all people, and its consequences. Jesus made the ultimate sacrifice because of a love that drove him to question and even to defy the accepted customs (context) of life in his society. In doing so, he incited the hatred of religious and political authorities of his time. His choices created a "moral loneliness" that put him outside the "context" of his society and on the cross, a loneliness voiced in the cry, "My God, my God, why have you forsaken me."

Jesus died for others, and in doing so, challenged his culture's—and our culture's—self-centeredness. We realize that as Christians, we too, are called to make difficult decisions that might cause us to be hated or rejected by the socio-political-religious establishment of our time. Perhaps the interpretation of Jesus' atonement in the gospel of Mark—living sacrificially for others and taking risks for our moral decisions comes closest to the Christian experience in our modern culture. Like Jesus, we too, might at first pray for the cup of sacrifice to pass us by. But when we choose to follow him and live a life that may sometimes cast us outside the context of our society, we are united with all Christians from all times and cultural contexts who have made the same choice.

This is reflected in our living out of the Last Supper, our shared belief that whenever we take the bread and wine, we are connected to the sacrifice of Jesus . . . and connected to all others in the context of this believing community, a context that is spiritual rather than cultural. Then, we realize the broader concept of "context" and its relationship to sacrifice. It is one that offers the power of renewal, thanksgiving, and challenge—the complete atonement.

The Gospel of Mark

The kingdom of God in Mark has to do with God's sovereign rule over the earth, which has come and will come on the last day.[14] The phrase "the kingdom of God" appears fourteen times in Mark, and the famous one is in Mark 1:15: "The time is fulfilled, and the kingdom of God has come near; repent, and believe in the good news." The kingdom of God (Greek genitive) has two meaning possibilities: a kingdom belonging to God and God's kingdom. The latter is called the subjective genitive; God is the subject of the kingdom. God as king reigns over the world. It is God's sovereign rule over the earth. But this sovereignty of God is not forceful to humans. To make this kingdom a reality, repentance (change of heart or turn to God) is needed, and people have to trust the good news of God. In Mark, this new

14. Tolbert, "Mark." See also Keener, *The Historical Jesus of the Gospels*, 197.

world that God rules will come soon on earth: "Truly I tell you, there are some standing here who will not taste death until they see that the kingdom of God has come with power" (Mark 9:1; cf. Mark 14:25 and 15:43).

In this Gospel, qualifications for participating in the kingdom of God in the now and the future are described in Mark 9:35–37 and 10:43–46. In the former Jesus says: "Whoever wants to be first must be last of all and servant of all. Whoever welcomes one such child in my name welcomes me, whoever welcomes me welcomes not me but the one who sent me." In the latter Jesus says: "Whoever wishes to be first among you must be slave of all. For the Son of Man came not to be served but to serve, and to give his life as ransom for many." Jesus' giving his life a ransom is not to be understood as atonement for the forgiveness of sinners; rather, it is to be a cost of service and justice. Advocating of God's kingdom needs a price. Jesus' costly life has a redemptive power for those who struggle with their faith in God in the Empire. People in this community undergoing persecution, are tempted to live by the power of the kingdom of Rome but are challenged to live with the ideal of the kingdom of God. The growth of the kingdom of God is like a mustard seed, which is initially unnoticeably small but has power hidden in it. When it grows, the birds make nests in its shade (Mark 4:31–32).

The Gospel of Matthew

The Gospel of Matthew is a most Jewish Gospel as Jesus affirms the place of Jewish law: "Do not think that I have come to abolish the law or the prophets; I have come not to abolish but to fulfill" (Matt 5:17). "God's righteousness" is a key theme in the Hebrew Bible and is emphasized in this Gospel along with God's kingdom: "But strive first for the kingdom of God and his righteousness, and all these things will be given to you as well" (Matt 6:33).[15] Jesus also explains that his baptism is necessary because of righteousness: "For it is proper for us in this way to fulfill all righteousness" (Matt 3:15). As stated before, "the kingdom of heaven" in Matthew is exchangeable with the kingdom of God. Taken together, the kingdom of God in Matthew is similar to the Markan Gospel. It refers to both God's sovereign rule in the present (Matt 6:33; 12:28) and a future kingdom of God on the last day (Matt 18:3).[16] God's kingdom has come: "Repent, for the

---

15. Holladay, *A Critical Introduction to the New Testament*, 152.

16. Westerholm, "Matthew." Some scholars make a distinction between the kingdom

kingdom of heaven has come near" (Matt 3:2) but yet to come completely, as we see from a final judgment scene (Matt 25:31–46).

But the clear difference with Mark is that Matthew has an emphasis on righteousness. A right action of the law is based on the love of God and the love of the neighbor (Matt 22:36–40). Jesus does not repeal the law but reinterprets it more contextually and ethically than the religious leaders at the time, so that the purpose of the law (God's righteousness) can be fulfilled in their lives (Matt 5:17). Thus Jesus says: "Not everyone who says to me, 'Lord, Lord,' will enter the kingdom of heaven, but only the one who does the will of my Father in heaven" (Matt 7:21).

The primary issue in Matthew's community is hypocrisy or incongruence between teaching and action.[17] Jesus says you have to learn what Pharisees teach but do not do what they do. Who can enter the kingdom of God or who can live according to God's rule? They are those who keep the law on the basis of the love of God and the love of the neighbor, as Jesus summarizes the entire law and prophets with the double commands (Matt 22:37–39). In beatitudes, Jesus teaches that the kingdom of God is for those who are poor in spirit (Matt 5:3), for those who are persecuted for righteousness' sake (Matt 5:10), and for those who do the will of the father in heaven (Matt 7:21). "Poor in spirit" should not mean a dualism between the body and the spirit; rather, it means a total devotion and search for God who wants his righteousness to be an everyday reality. Those who strive for God's kingdom are persecuted but are the blessed ones. God's kingdom is not coming by word only but by word and action.

The Gospel of Luke

In Luke, the kingdom of God is primarily the present one and worked out through healing and restoration of God's family.[18] The emphasis of the Lukan Gospel is global mission and the Spirit's activities in the world.[19] No imminent end of the world is expected or emphasized and *Parousia* (coming of the Lord) is delayed. The Pharisees ask Jesus when the kingdom of God

of God and the kingdom of heaven. The former applies to the ministry of Jesus and the latter to the final consummation in the future. See Walker, "Kingdom of the Son of Man," 574. See also Patte, "The Kingdom of God," 690.

17. Westerholm, "Matthew."

18. Carroll, "Luke," 701.

19. Holladay, *A Critical Introduction to the New Testament*, 178–81.

is coming, and Jesus answers: "The kingdom of God is not coming with things that can be observed; nor will they say, 'Look, here it is! or 'There it is!' For, in fact, the kingdom of God is among you" (Luke 17:20–21). The delay of *Parousia* is understandable and needed for the people in Lukan community who have to adapt to the new social political situation under the Roman Empire, seeking the survival and growth of the church. Naturally, the message of this Gospel tends to underscore the present realization of God's work in the world. In Luke, as we saw before in Matthew and Mark, the concept of the kingdom of God is similar to the other synoptic Gospels: God's sovereignty over earth (Luke 6:20; 9:2, 60) and a future kingdom of God (Luke 22:16, 18). God's sovereign rule has come already (Luke 10:9, 11; 11:20).

Who can participate in the kingdom of God? Those who are like little children (Luke 18:16–17) and those who share what they have with others (not like the rich who do not share) can enjoy the life of God's kingdom. Jesus teaches that the kingdom of God is for those who are poor (Luke 6:20). This is a difficult teaching. Even though the poor are now poor, they are to be blessed in the kingdom of God. In other words, the existence of the poor is not possible in God's sovereign rule on earth. This teaching of Luke 6:20 "Blessed are you who are poor, for yours is the kingdom of God" is a challenge to those who have more than they need, because all are to be blessed in the kingdom of God. The rich will find it difficult to enter the kingdom of God not because of wealth itself but because they do not share with the poor (Luke 18:24–25). The kingdom of God as God's sovereign rule on earth is for all people, the poor and the rich. In order for the poor to be blessed, there must be a redistribution of goods and wealth. That is what Jesus says the poor are blessed not because they are poor but because they are to be blessed.

In sum, the synoptic Gospels have similar views of the kingdom of God: God's sovereign rule on earth and the future kingdom of God that is yet to come completely. Jesus is the messiah, the Son of God, who preaches and lives for the realization of the kingdom of God in the midst of all chaos and injustices. But differences among the Gospels are due to the different needs of each Gospel community. For example, Matthew emphasizes a more Jewish side of the Gospel in that Jesus is a new teacher who re-interprets God's law on the basis of the love of God and the love of the neighbor. Jesus affirms Jewish law and renews Jewish life by demanding the congruence between what they believe about God (or the law) and what they act. Mark emphasizes a suffering side of the messiah who challenges the wisdom of the world that oppresses God's people and who empowers fearing Christians to follow the footsteps of Jesus. In that way, the rule of God is realized sooner or later. Luke, given the delay of *Parousia*, shifts its focus to the present world mission. To realize this goal, Luke presents a new sharing ethics that the kingdom of God is coming through people who participate in the Spirit.

The Gospel of John

The Gospel of John is very different from the synoptic Gospels in several ways.[20] For example, we do not find Jesus' baptism, passion narrative or parables. Some suggest that this Gospel reflects the Johannine community's schism with the synagogue in the late first century CE. That is why the language of this Gospel is markedly different from the synoptic Gospels. In Christian tradition, this Gospel has been highly cherished because of its emphasis on "spiritual gospel," and we easily find related Johannine key theological vocabulary such as Logos, symbols/metaphors of eternal life, light, and darkness. So much so this Gospel has been read as guarantee-ing individual salvation by believing in Jesus. Likewise, simple belief in Jesus paves the way to the heavenly places. Jesus goes to prepare a heavenly dwelling place for believers. So Jesus is the only way to heaven, an immortal life. Exclusivism begins here.

But the Gospel of John can be read very differently from the above if we locate this community in a particular context where people are strug-gling with their isolated identity due to a recent split with the synagogues. The kingdom of God in this Gospel is not very much different from the synoptic Gospels. It still refers to God's sovereign rule on earth, which comes from the mission of the Logos as clearly stated in the Prologue (John 1:1–18). Jesus as the Logos is sent by God to bring the life and light to the world. It is God's mission that Jesus obeys. But the world (darkness) does not accept the life and light. If the life and light is good to the world, the world should accept it. That is an irony. The world does not embrace the message of Jesus because people dwelling in darkness do not want to be exposed to the light. So God's mission of the Logos is opposed, and Jesus is

---

20. Lee, "John." See also Holladay, *A Critical Introduction to the New Testament*, 191–202.

hated and persecuted. For Jesus, there is no other way than walking the way of life and light coming from God.

Even though the contents or focus of God's sovereignty in this gospel is different from the synoptic Gospels, what is clear in this Gospel is God's initiative in this world, expressed with the calling of the Logos. Jesus, the incarnate Son of God, is carrying out this initiative throughout the Johannine narrative. Jesus never sees himself as separate from God the Father. Even when he says that God and he are one, he does not mean that he is God but that they are working closely (the unity of working relationship).

Now let us see two occurrences of the kingdom of God in John's Gospel: "Jesus answered him, 'very truly, I tell you, no one can enter the kingdom of God without being born from above'" (John 3:3); ". . . no one can enter the kingdom of God without being born of water and Spirit" (John 3:4). These two occurrences occur in Jesus' answer to Nicodemus who came to Jesus to ask about his teaching and authority. In order to understand the meaning of the kingdom of God here, we have to read the whole Gospel where Jesus as the Logos incarnate appears to emphasize the eternal abiding relationship with God, which is achieved now and going forever. That is the "eternal life" that Jesus talks about. Jesus says to Martha: "I am the resurrection" in the present tense. Likewise, "I am the way, the truth, the life" (John 14:6). Though Jesus talks about the future tense of resurrection or the kingdom of God, similar to the synoptic Gospels, the primary focus of his message is the present tense. Jesus is the present embodiment of God's presence. He is the incarnate Son of God now. He is the one who makes sure that God's sovereignty is realized in the hostile world.

In conversation with Nicodemus, Jesus says the kingdom of God is not something like a physical birth that Nicodemus observes by his eyes and experience. Jesus talks about a birth from above (*anothen* in Greek means two things: "above" or "again"). This birth from above is not like a one time birth or physical birth. Why is this reading possible? I will explain using the translation of the Greek adverb *anothen*, which is central to our understanding about spiritual birth. In the episode of Nicodemus' conversation with Jesus (John 3:1–10), we see the Greek adverb *anothen* in 3:3 and 7.

In response to Nicodemus' statement that "'Rabbi, we know that you are a teacher who has come from God; for no one can do these signs that you do apart from the presence of God," Jesus answers: "No one can see the kingdom of God without being born *anothen*" (3:3). In 3:7 as well we see:

"Do not be astonished that I said to you, 'You must be born *anothen*.'" By
the way, *anothen* means "from above" or "again (anew)." What is the best
translation and why? Before we choose which translation is best, let us see
what is going on here between these two figures. When Jesus answers that
"no one can enter the kingdom of God without being born *anothen*," Jesus
could mean one or the other, or both. Jesus means the birth from above,
as he talks about the spiritual birth (3:6: "born of water and spirit"). Jesus
also talks about the character of a spiritual person like the wind blowing.
Jesus could mean also another birth (anew) that emphasizes "new kind of
birth" (similar to spiritual birth) because of the spiritual connection with
God (the Spirit). If we understand this way, "born from above" and "born
anew" are not separate; because the born above person is also living a new
birth. New birth is possible because of one's connection with God ("from
above"). But what is not the case here is that Jesus does not mean a one-
time spiritual birth like physical birth. Even though Jesus says a new kind of
birth (so again or anew), it is to be understood as "the above" (from God),
as Jesus as the Logos comes from above. The way of new life is to accept the
Logos, coming from above.

Now Nicodemus responds a bit comically and answers "'how can anyone be born after having grown old? Can one enter a second time into the
mother's womb and be born?'" (3:4). Nicodemus certainly misunderstands
him. So Jesus once again answers clearly: "'Very truly, I tell you, no one can
enter the kingdom of God without being born of water and Spirit. What
is born of the flesh is flesh, and what is born of the Spirit is spirit" (3:5–6).
This time Jesus explains about the person born from above (or anew)
through the different language "born of water and Spirit." Although difficult to know what water and Spirit have to do with new birth, in my view,
water stands for physical birth (water of womb), and Spirit is the Spirit
of God. In other words, here Jesus' emphasis would be that everybody is
born naturally (born of water) but that is not enough. One more birth is
needed, which is born of the Spirit (from God). Jesus emphasizes two births
simultaneously; that is what humanity is, ideally. Jesus further clarifies two
births: "What is born of the flesh is flesh; what is born of the Spirit is spirit."
This view is consistent with the theme of Johannine literature (community): Jesus' identity as coming with flesh and working through the Spirit.
The two are not opposing each other but need each other. Flesh dwelled
among us (John 1:14). Seen here, "water" symbolizes the essential birth
of physicality. One more birth is needed to complete what humans are in

relation to God and the world. Furthermore, Jesus qualifies the character of the person born from above (or anew). He or she is like the wind (or spirit) in the sense that the wind blows anywhere; so the identity or source is not known until the actual work is seen. Wind blows continually so the spiritual person continues to work like the wind without emphasizing his or her name or identity. But unfortunately, the NIV translation translates the Greek "anothen" as "again" in 3:3 and 3:7. This is problematic because the popular idea of the second birth is fixed one time like a physical birth.

We have covered so far that God's kingdom in John's Gospel can be understood as the realm of God who brings the life and light to the world through Jesus, the incarnate Son of God. Let us focus now on the believers' side. Who can enter the kingdom of God? Those who are born from above can enter and they are those who continue in Jesus' word (John 8:31). His word is none other than all about the mission of the Logos. We know that Jesus taught a difficult teaching to his disciples who responded to him: "This teaching is difficult; who can accept it?" (John 6:60). His teaching is about other-centered love and sacrifice: "Those who eat my flesh and drink my blood have eternal life" (John 6:54). That is his teaching. Simply, the way of God's life and light is to follow the difficult teaching of Jesus.

Paul's Seven Undisputed Letters

Even though Paul does not frequently use the phrase "the kingdom of God" (six verses only in the seven undisputed letters), the overall meaning of the phrase is consistent with the four canonical Gospels. That is, the kingdom of God is God's sovereign rule and the future kingdom of God that is yet to come. Regarding the former, Paul says in Rom 14:17 for example: "For the kingdom of God is not food and drink but righteousness and peace and joy in the Holy Spirit." Here Paul talks about the quality of life in the community where God's righteousness, peace, and joy are abundant. Likewise, 1 Cor 4:20 states: "For the kingdom of God depends not on talk but on power." Regarding the latter, Paul has a clear vision of a future kingdom of God, just like any Jewish contemporaries, when God's messianic age will be complete. So Paul refers to the kingdom of God that is coming in the future: "Wrongdoers will not inherit the kingdom of God" (1 Cor 6:9–10; cf. Gal 5:21); "flesh and blood cannot inherit the kingdom of God" (1 Cor 15:50).

Even though Paul does not use the phrase "the kingdom of God" as frequently as the canonical Gospels, his theology of God's righteousness (*dikaiosyne theou*, Rom 1:17; 3:21–26) is similar to God's kingdom (Rom 1:17; 3:21–26); as for Paul, God's righteousness is understood as God's character and action toward humanity.[21] It is God's sovereign rule on earth. How is this rule of God, according to Paul, available? It is by Christ's faith, not by the believer's faith. Christ Jesus is the one who shows who God is and what God wants: peace, life, and justice (Rom 8:6; 14:17). The believer's job is to participate in Christ's faith: "God's righteousness through Christ's faith for all who believe" (Rom 3:22).[22] "For all who believe" does not refer to accepting what Jesus had done for the believer but refer to participating in his faith, life, and death. The Greek verb *pisteuo* is close to the meaning of loyalty or trust. This participation of the believer is further emphasized through the body metaphor: "You are Christ-like body" (1 Cor 12:27).[23]

The Deutero-Pauline and Pastoral Letters

Surprisingly, when it comes to the Deutero-Pauline and Pastoral Letters, the kingdom of God appears only twice (Col 4:11; 2 Thess 1:5). Furthermore, theology found in these letters is very much removed from the earlier writings that we studied so far (Gospels and Paul's letters). Here God is seen as hierarchical, the teaching is doctrinal, the church becomes rigidly structured with hierarchical offices, and salvation is once and for all and otherworldly. The kingdom of God is no more this worldly but otherworldly. Faith is belief. Paul's message of participatory faith in Christ is hardly found. Christ's faith is hardly found either. Christ's sacrifice as sin offering is a price for sinners (Eph 5:2; Col 1:14, 20). Christian identity is already firmly established, and the believers were already raised up with Christ in the heavenly places (Eph 2:6; Col 3:1–4).

Thus far, we have seen complexities of the kingdom of God in the Hebrew Scriptures and the New Testament. Oftentimes, the message of the phrase is not consistent, conflicting with each other. Nonetheless, there is a grand stream of theology focused on the messianic fulfillment of the kingdom of God, whether now on earth or somewhere else in the future. Overall, what we learned is that the central message of the synoptic Gospels is "repent, the kingdom of God is at hand." Even in the Gospel of John, "believe in me" is accepting the cost and work of the Logos that brings

21. Kim, *A Theological Introduction to Paul's Letters*, 53–62.

22. Ibid.

23. Kim, *Christ's Body in Corinth*.

oppositions and hatred from the world. Of course, the New Testament does not speak about a single vision of the kingdom of God, and all differences should not be harmonized. Each testimony should be considered on its own, and we can learn both pros and cons of a particular testimony. That is where we have to move to the next section, *Engagement with the Kingdom of God*. That is, the question is how we evaluate different readings of the kingdom of God and what stance we take.

Engagement with "the Kingdom of God"

Thus far we have explored the world of the reader and the world of the text with a focus on "the kingdom of God." In fact, we cannot separate the text from the reader and vice versa. We will see below a few readings of the kingdom of God employed in biblical interpretation and analyze them. The question is what kind of reading of the kingdom of God is the best for our lives today.

God's Reign of Justice as the Kingdom of God

God's reign of justice as the kingdom of God considers God's character of justice as the most important realization of the kingdom of God in the world—God's reign on earth.[24] The eighth century BCE prophets such as Amos and Micah cry for the justice of society. Micah says: "He has told you, O mortal, what is good; and what does the LORD require of you but to do justice, and to love kindness, and to walk humbly with your God?" (Micah 6:8). Similarly, according to Amos, the Lord says: "I hate, I despise your festivals, and I take no delight in your solemn assemblies. . . . Take away from the noise of your songs. . . . But let justice roll down like waters, and righteousness like an ever-flowing stream" (Amos 5:21–24). God is concerned about the poor and the marginalized. Jesus is believed to preach the same message of the prophets. Jesus proclaims that the kingdom of God has come and that people have to repent to embody God's justice in society. Those who emphasize the political, social justice in the world follow this reading.[25] The role of God is clear and important. God is the one who is

24. Chilton and Mcdonald show that the kingdom of God is performative and humans also need to participate in God's performance of the reign of justice. See *Jesus and the Ethics of the Kingdom*, 24–31. See also Stassen and Gushee, *Kingdom Ethics*, 21.

25. Borg, *Conflict, Holiness, and Politics in the Teaching of Jesus*; also, *Jesus; Meeting*

just and loves humanity equally. Jesus embodies God's presence through his faith. Likewise, the believers are to live like Christ in bringing God's justice in the world. This reading has many advocates: liberation theologians, feminists, and other practitioners of social justice. Perhaps the main weakness of this reading is the lack of human transformation in terms of personal change in relation to the world. External social conditions must be addressed and transformed but at the same time personal changes must be brought together, because ultimately the real change must begin with persons in the world.

Apocalyptic Reality of a New World as the Kingdom of God

This reading of "apocalyptic reality of a new world as the kingdom of God" emphasizes the timeline of the kingdom of God.[26] That is, the completion of the kingdom of God is yet to come. The historical Jesus might have followed this line. Albert Schweitzer's view of Jesus is that of the apocalyptic Jesus who anticipated the end of the world and the new world in his life. There must be a new world that replaces the old. That is the only way that guarantees the kingdom of God, which is the state of the kingdom, not God's rule. Similarly, the Qumran community withdrawn to the desert expected the radical intervention of God when a new world starts according to their vision. From a Jewish perspective, this kind of kingdom of God is not distinguishable from the messianic age when God will establish a new time and kingdom centered on the Jewish nation to which all nations flock to worship in Jerusalem. The Book of Revelation is also good evidence that the hope is the future coming of the kingdom of God (Rev 11:15; 22:20).

But even in this view of the apocalyptic reality of the kingdom of God there are different views about how to wait for this finalization of the kingdom. What can people do? This question is exactly the one that divided the Jews in their responses to personal, communal, and national crises due to the foreign invasion and domination under the Roman Empire and also due to the corrupt leadership of Jerusalem. For example, the Qumran community expected God to radically intervene in history and therefore withdrew to a desert, forming an ascetic, strict rules-abiding community.

Jesus Again for the First Time; and with N. T. Wright, *The Meaning of Jesus*. See Crossan, *The Birth of Christianity*; *The Historical Jesus*; *In Parables*; and *Jesus*.

26. Schweitzer, *The Mystery of Kingdom of God*; and *The Quest of the Historical Jesus*. See also Allison, "The Eschatology of Jesus"; and *Jesus of Nazareth*.

In contrast, the Pharisees worked hard in society by teaching the law to ascertain that they were ready to enter the kingdom of God. Still, the other group of people waged armed resistance against Rome and believed that God's new world would be coming soon. Where does Jesus stand in the milieu of first-century Palestine? It seems that Jesus is neither like the Qumran community who withdrew to the desert nor like the armed group of people. As we see from the story of cleansing of the temple, Jesus' action was violent enough; he turned the table of moneychangers upside down. His action is symbolic yet violent and hints a new world order with the renewed temple.

Overall, in this apocalyptic reading, the role of God is not very clear except for God's radical intervention on the last day. The role of Jesus is limited to the proclamation of the apocalyptic message of judgment and the end of the world. In order to avoid the judgment, people have to serve one of the least of these (Mt 25:31–46). God's wrath incurs because of human disobedience to God (Rom 2–3). The solution is to have the faith of Jesus. The strong point of this reading is that God's justice ultimately prevails. The implication is that the believers must endure through faith in God. The main weakness is, however, the de-emphasis of this world that needs transformation. Because the apocalyptic gospel focuses on a sudden end of the world in the future, the tendency is to see this world as a transitory place. Moreover, along with this sudden end, violence is legitimated as Jesus brings violence to judge the world.[27]

The Church as the Kingdom of God

In this reading the church serves as embodying the kingdom of God.[28] This church community comprises of the believers who share Jesus' self-sacrificing love in the world. The foundation of the church is Christ's life, death, and resurrection. Jesus embodies the kingdom of God in his life.[29] The church continues his ministry, and provides an alternative vision to the world by living differently from the world. In this sense, the church must be

---

27. Part of the historical Jesus debate is over the view of Jesus: the apocalyptic Jesus vs. the sapiential Jesus. The latter refers to a teacher of wisdom who teaches to transform the world. Marcus Borg and John D. Crossan for example advocate this position. See Miller (ed.), *The Apocalyptic Jesus*, 163.

28. Gingerich, "The Church as Kingdom," 129–43.

29. See Hauweras, *Against the Nations*, 116. Hauerwas and Willimon, *Resident Aliens*, 17. See also Yoder, *The Christian Witness to the State*, 8–9.

a minority community, separating itself from others.[30] Here the role of God is justice and liberation of the people. Yet God's kingdom is fundamentally different from the kingdom of the world. In this regard, this reading is different from a liberal version of the kingdom of God that may cooperate with the world institutions. God is benevolent, patient, and pacifist. Jesus is a model to follow especially in his non-violent work to embody God's kingdom in the world. The believers are to work through a special community called the church. This kingdom of God is yet to come fully, but the church must continue to work on this until it is completed in the future. The strong point of this reading lies in the realistic and prophetic understanding of the role of the church—the church as a minority prophetic institution that can lead society. The weakness of this reading lies in the scope of agents for the kingdom of God. That is, agents can be diversely many others and institutions more than the church.

Personal Experience of God's Grace as the Kingdom of God

What is emphasized here is the individual experience of God's grace and reign. The kingdom of God is experienced individually in one's relationship with God and neighbors. God is so graceful. In the gospel stories, Jesus is a model of intimate relationship with God. In Deutero-Pauline and Pastorals, Christ is a means of sacrifice for the forgiveness of sins. The believers are reconciled with God because of Christ's sacrifice focused on the sin offering. The strong point is to embrace an individual's personal connection with God and to feel strong identity in Christ. But the price is very high. Christ's role is minimized; Christ only came to die to pay the price of sins. Otherwise, there is no emphasis of Christ's faith that ended up with a cross. In other words, if Jesus' message of the kingdom of God had succeeded and people had repented, Jesus could not have been crucified. His crucifixion is a result of his faith that boldly proclaimed God's kingdom that was opposed and rejected by the political and religious leaders in his time. It is not our faith in Christ that saved us from all burdens but his faith in God showed who God is and makes us participate in his life and death (that is what Paul calls Christ's faith, *pistis christou*; Rom 3:21–22).[31] Our faith is to have his faith. Our righteousness is not the point of Paul's message; for Paul, it is

---

30. Yoder, *The Politics of Jesus*, 23; *The Priestly Kingdom*; *The Royal Priesthood*; and *For the Nations*.

31. Kim, *A Theological Introduction to Paul's Letters*, 63–82.

4333333333333333

always God's righteousness that is manifest in the world through Christ's faith (Rom 3:21). Our role as Christians is to have his faith, which means dying for God's righteousness.

Summary

The question is which interpretation of the kingdom of God is the best in what context. Though each different reading may work in a particular context, it does not mean that it is an absolute reading that does not need other readings. For example, the kingdom of God may be understood as the personal experience of God's grace, but that should not exclude other aspects of the kingdom of God that emphasize the socio-political or apocalyptic dimensions of God's kingdom. The best interpretation must consider and include the various aspects of the kingdom of God as we sketched before. However, the best interpretation should not be fossilized or absolutized once and for all. A particular best interpretation should be constructed each time, deconstructed, and reconstructed next time, because each situation of the reader (or the community) calls for a new contextual meaning. For instance, at one time as unjust society is an issue, social justice or the community aspect of God's kingdom will be emphasized. But this does not mean that there is no other message of God's kingdom. The personal or apocalyptic message of God's kingdom may complement the understanding of social justice because the meaning of social justice may be enriched because of this association with other aspects of the kingdom. For example, personal suffering of the pain due to illness or any other troubles can become a moment of prayerful engagement and discernment of the world that he or she yearns for. Then our understanding of the kingdom of God can be balanced between the present and future, and between personal experience and communal experience. If a person is in despair due to an incurable disease, the primary emphasis of the kingdom of God may be personal in the sense that the kingdom of God is like God's presence now and in the future. There will be assurance and comfort because God is in charge of an ultimate destiny of ours. Here the good news of the kingdom of God is: "You are the children of God; God will take care of you." In another situation where a person is seriously wrong with Christian responsibility or moral behavior, the message of the kingdom of God must be different. Now good news in this situation is: "You cannot enter the kingdom of God unless you repent." Good news here is not a sweet word of comfort but a harsh judgment or warning.

The criteria for the best interpretation of the kingdom of God are similar to those criteria discussed in chapter 5: critical diversity and solidarity, congruence, and balance. The first criterion of critical diversity and solidarity helps us focus on both the diversity of the kingdom of God and the solidarity of the kingdom for all people. On the one hand, the diverse aspects of God's kingdom are to be considered, and on the other hand, the purpose of God's kingdom is to be focused on the welfare of all people. Congruence of interpretation means that there must be agreement between textuality and contextuality in terms of the need and solution, so that the kingdom of God may address a particular situation even though it does not exclude other aspects of the kingdom. Balance of interpretation means that there are to be various sets of balances for example between person and community, between the present and the future, and between love and justice. Ultimately, the task of the reader is not simply what the Bible says but what we read in/from the Bible. In order to do this job, we should shun over-historicizing of the text or over-contextualizing of the reader without fully engaging the text from a diversity of perspectives.

In this chapter we explored a daunting task of interpreting and evaluating the kingdom of God from the perspective of a critical contextual interpretation that involves the three elements of interpretation: the reader, the text, and engagement ("theological lens"). Theoretically, there is no one ideal interpretation that covers all situations of the reader but a number of interpretations that tell different things in different contexts. But even with this much of variety or diversity of interpretations, which are certainly celebratory, not all interpretations are equally valid. In fact, some readings may be so naïve or shallow that the reader does not fully consider the historical context and his or her life context. In this regard, interpretation is a business of engagement between the present and the past, or between today's readers and ancient readers. With this process of engagement, I propose that the best interpretation should at least include some or all of the criteria that we explored in chapter 5.

Questions for Further Reflection

1. In your view, what are the most important issues facing humanity or Christians in particular, as you contemplate on the kingdom of God?

2. Read the two accounts of creation in Gen 1–2, and discuss meaning of human beings in terms of the purpose of human life in the world.

3. How do we understand human suffering or vulnerability of human lives as we think of the kingdom of God?

4. A mega-church can be evidence of failure of a mission started by Jesus. Do you agree?

5. When and why is the kingdom (*malkuth* in Hebrew) introduced and emphasized in the Hebrew Scriptures? Include times of prosperity and suffering.

6. Does the New Testament continue the tradition of the kingdom of God portrayed in the Hebrew Scriptures? Talk about some aspects of continuity and some aspects of discontinuity.

7. Discuss the different uses of the kingdom of God in the New Testament. How is each Gospel different? Compare with Paul's letters. How is the kingdom of God in Paul's letters different from the so-called Deutero-Pauline and Pastorals?

8. Compare the historical Jesus' teaching about the kingdom of God. Is his teaching continued in the canonical Gospels? If different, what is his primary teaching about it?

9. Is the historical Jesus' message of the kingdom of God primarily apocalyptic or sapiential?

10. What is the kingdom of God for you? Address specific issues about the kingdom of God. Discuss pros and cons of a few readings of the kingdom of God: God's reign of justice as the kingdom of God, apocalyptic reality of a new world as the kingdom of God, the church as the kingdom of God, and personal experience of God's grace as the kingdom of God.

11. How can you relate Jesus' death to the kingdom of God? Relationships?

Chapter Seven

Conclusion

We have explored theory, process, and criteria of biblical interpretation, which involves the text, the reader, and the theological lens. We also have explored ways of reading the kingdom of God as a test case for critical contextual interpretation. The bottom line is that the reader makes a final meaning by bringing to the text his or her worldview, issues, and life experience, through which the given text is well illuminated, and vice versa. The reader engages the text through a particular reading lens in a certain life context. The real reader of the world today has to decide how the given text makes sense.

However, oftentimes we are told to distance ourselves from the text as if the most authentic or original meaning could be excavated like archaeological finds. That view is a kind of delusion because even the archaeological finds do not tell us of something obvious about the past; rather, they should be interpreted. Often we teach and learn as if we were not out of this world or for this world. Even though we learn and teach source theory of the Pentateuch or the synoptic Gospels, the point of lesson is not to teach the precision of theory but the implication of that theory and ramifications for our life today. Whichever text we read, it does not tell us of everything that we need in our lives. More or less, what we have is a composite of various testimonies of people's religious experience.

Because God cannot be stuck in a book or in anyone's interpretation and the Spirit is present here and now on earth, we the real readers continue to grapple with meaning of God and the world today, in its most complex life situations. Likewise, when it comes to biblical authority, the reader's constant engaging of the text is crucial, and biblical authority is to be endlessly constructed and deconstructed so that we may experience blessings of God that do not discriminate any one on the basis of any sort. Actually, scriptures are the result of the long process of faith people who engage in constructing and reconstructing of their traditions in new life contexts. Without their critical or faithful role of the reader, we would not have inherited bulks of scriptures that had been written and re-written, edited and re-edited throughout history. That kind of the reader's history and interpretation continues even today.

Given the important role of the reader as such, biblical interpretation should give more attention to the study of the real readers in the world. For example, human sciences such as anthropology, ecology or psychology will be helpful for that purpose. Clarification and realization of who we are in the world not only helps us to understand ancient texts, but also to engage them critically and faithfully. Toward that purpose of a new reading I would like to recommend the following tips:

- Healthy biblical theology or biblical interpretation begins with the reader's critical self-consciousness by which I mean he or she should engage the real world from every bit of perspective in his or her life.

- The issue of biblical interpretation is not merely what the Bible says but what we say about it—discerning what is good or acceptable to God and to the neighbor.

- Biblical texts, both historical and theological, are to be interpreted through a critical imagination that engages both mind and heart.

In all of this, the ultimate question is: How do we know which interpretation is the best or better than the other? Even though multiple interpretations are plausible, not all of them are equally valid or helpful. Some might work in certain contexts but may not work in other contexts. Some reading may be harmful to other people in other contexts. That is where we need to discuss criteria for solid interpretation. I suggested that solid interpretation should be based on the following: the critical diversity and solidarity, congruence of interpretation, and balance of interpretation. Critical diversity means that different life experiences or different theology should be honored and yet evaluated against the holistic aspects of life. This critical diversity leads to solidarity. Congruence of interpretation means an agreement between life context and view of the text. Simply, the root cause of a lack of knowledge can be resolved by the view of the text as "a lamp-to-my-feet." Balance of interpretation means that interpretation should address the balanced aspects of human life; for example, the inter-relation between self, neighbor, and God are to be considered for deciding a solid interpretation. As a test case of critical interpretation, we examined the kingdom of God.

In the end, good biblical interpretation is the one that involves per-spectives of diversity, approaches of balance, and growth of holism. As God made the world and us with diversity, we also have to see ourselves through the perspective of diversity. We have to embrace the diversity of cultures, experiences, and various dimensions of human lives. Because of this kind of diversity, we need to use the approach of balance, a balance between head and heart, between critical and self-critical approaches to the text and our human lives. Through the diversity perspective and the balanced ap-proach, we can aim at holistic growth that involves not only the intellectual, emotional, and performative element of our lives but also diverse aspects of lives: personal and public, individual and communal, local and global, religious and political. My last question is: How can we read the Bible dif-ferently if we are informed by diversity, balance, and holism?

Before closing, I illustrate my own approach to the text. *I read the Bible from a Korean multicultural perspective, which reflects a bit of who I am as a multi-cultural, border person.* I have a passion for human transfor-mation, rooted in self-knowledge and self-criticism. Traveling many Latin American countries during my business career, I learned a great deal about cultural diversity and the need of human solidarity. With a new vocation of theological education, I now ask: What does it mean to live in this world in relation to each other (i.e., meaning of the Other — which resonates Emmanuel Levinas' "the face of the other," Paul Ricoeur's inter-subjective narrative identity, or Jacques Derrida's "relationless relation"), and How can we do theology in our thoughts, deeds and action, while moving pointedly away from individualism? How can we read biblical stories with each other in a critical context? What are some viable definitions of cross-cultural hermeneutics, if any, by which we can improve the sense of living together in difference?

With this new journey of my life, I approach the Bible through the lens of human transformation, based on *kenosis*. Let me illustrate it. Once upon a time there were a father and his son; they were beggars. One day just across a river a big fire broke out and saw a big house being burnt down by the fire. The father said to his son proudly, "My son, we are so fortunate because we do not have a house to be burnt down." This comic but pithy conversation speaks of some lessons about our life; our happiness does not rest on material things.

Similarly, Christian understanding of *kenosis* (Phil 2:6–11, emptying of oneself) reflects nothingness attitude in our life. It is also found in the Q gospel: There was once a rich man whose lands yielded a good harvest. He thought: "What should I do? I don't have enough room to store my crops. I know, I'll tear down my barns and build bigger ones so that I can keep all my grain in them. Then I will say to myself, 'I have enough to last me for years. I can take it easy, eat, drink and have a good time.'" But God said to him, "You fool! This very night you may die. Then who will own this hoard of yours? So it is with those who pile up possessions but remain poor in the treasures of the spirit." Jesus says, "If you try to gain your life, you will lose it; but if you lose it, you will gain it." Similarly, Paul says: "I die everyday on the cross." If you gather more and more and do not give out, you will become slaves of riches. But if you give up more and more, your freedom of heart will be greater and greater. Furthermore, your self will live a meaningful life, a perfection of life with a sense of living with others in the community. In this way our life extends forever; it is not different from the idea of "eternal life" in the Gospel of John. True spirituality begins when we feel the same fate with others and act out by giving what we have. God wants a fair balance between the rich and the poor. God wants the light and life for all because God is the God of all.

Exactly, Jesus' ministry and his death can be understood as his testimony about God the Father. Bluntly speaking, if Jesus' preaching of the kingdom of God had been accepted by the people in his time, he would not have been executed. As the Gospel stories affirm, Jesus' crucifixion was the result of his costly message about the kingdom of God that undoes the status quo of society. In other words, his death is the culmination of what he spoke and acted against evil (social or political, Jerusalem and Rome included).[1] Jesus' claim of radical love and justice of God embraces the

1. See Borg, *The Heart of Christianity*, 80–100. Borg is committed to making Christianity viable and authentic for modern people by making distinction between the "old" paradigm and the "emerging" paradigm of Christianity. Borg is passionate about authentic Christian message rooted in Jesus and Paul, which is basically about living the transformative life. This book not only deconstructs the old paradigm but also reconstructs a more healthy way of living Christian life today without losing faith, hope and love of God. "Salvation is about the transformation of life, individually together, here and now. And the Bible speaks of these two transformations as an experience now, and as a hope for history, and as a hope that leads beyond history" (p. 183). In my book *Christ's Body in Corinth*, I continue the spirit of this kind of authentic faith and Christian experience. As

most vulnerable in society. Jesus was rejected and ended up on a cross not because he talked about the love of God but because he enacted the radical love of God. To evaluate the meaning of Jesus' death two excursuses follow.

Excursus: Jesus' death in the New Testament

Jesus' death attested in the Synoptic Gospels is not directly related to the forgiveness of sins. The forgiveness of sins is possible at baptism when people repent or when people forgive other people. For example, in the Lord's Prayer: "Forgive us as we forgive our debtors." God forgives people when they repent. John the Baptist and Jesus as well preached the same message: "Repent and the Kingdom of God has come." The kingdom message of John the Baptist and Jesus cost their lives. Jesus' death in the Synoptic Gospels implies a costly love. It also implies God's judgment (justice) against violence and injustices. Although Luke presents a politically innocuous gospel as we see in a centurion's confession at the crucifixion scene "Truly this man was innocent (*dikaios*)," Jesus' death in historical context involves political charges against the Roman Empire, because he proclaimed the kingdom of God, not the kingdom of Rome. But in Mark and Matthew, this same centurion says that "he was the Son of God" which connotes the work of God's Son, not the work of Caesar as the Son of God. As we saw before, even the Fourth Gospel has a similar view of Jesus' death with they Synoptic Gospels.

What about Paul's letters? It is Christ's faith (the subjective genitive of *pistis christou*) that caused his death. Christ's life and death should be read together along with the cause and effect. Even when we talk about Rom 3:25 where Paul uses the Greek word *hilasterion* which refers to God's act of sacrifice ("God put forward as a *hilasterion* by his blood"), the meaning of *hilasterion* does not necessarily refer to Christ's sin offering. In Hellenistic culture *hilasterion* means a propitiation, which has

---

for Paul, the center of the heart of his theology is "embodiment" of Christ. It is "Christic body." If we read Rom 8:1–11, what is essential for Paul is to live the faithful life of Christ, not a mere belief in Jesus but a life of faithful action modeled after Christ's cross. The central message here (Rom 8) is not something like "Jesus died instead of me or for sin; so I don't die." The opposite is true. Jesus died and I should die too. In other words, again in Rom 8:1–11, those who walk according to the Spirit are the ones who submit their will to God's law, which aims at "life and peace." I believe that Borg's sketch of authentic Christian faith aiming at transformation of our lives is very important to our re-envisioning of a new community for all.

to do with appeasing an angry god. *Hilasterion* is the Greek translation of the Hebrew *kapporeh*, which means covering or the cover of the ark (mercy seat) used on the Day of Atonement, *Yom Kippur* (Exod 25:10–22; 37:1–9). What does Paul mean by *hilasterion* here in Rom 3:25? Options are many: 1) Propitiation in the sense that Jesus' death appeases an angry God? 2) Or, is Jesus' death like sacrificial victims whose blood is sprinkled on the cover of the ark so that sins of people are covered? 3) A proper expiation (rectifying things) made? 4) Or, does Paul mean a mercy seat—God's holy presence right over there on the cross of Jesus because of Christ's faith? In my view, this last option makes more sense in the way that God affirms Jesus' faith.

The Gospels and Paul's letters (seven undisputed letters only) affirm the historically significant aspects of Jesus' death as stated before. But as time goes by, the cause of Jesus' death takes on another direction, far removed from the historical Jesus. For example, Hebrews presents Jesus' death referred to as the perfect sacrifice that replaces the animal sacrifice of the old covenant. In it Jesus himself is the High Priest, who becomes a new covenant; we see here some kind of supercessionism in which a new covenant replaces the old covenant, which is out of context if we read "a new covenant" in Jer 31:31–34 in a historical, literary context, because a new covenant in Jeremiah is made with the house of Israel and the house of Judah, not for later Christians.

In our world today, there are many sufferings, unjust or needless. I believe that God does not want our torturing. Jesus is a type of the most vicious and unjust suffering and death. This way of reading of Jesus' death is certainly plausible and one important avenue to look at the history and meaning of the event. In fact, the cause of Jesus' death could be constructed in many different ways, as the Four Gospels themselves in the New Testament testify. In Luke, Jesus' work as a prophet provokes enemies' anger. Jesus dies as a martyr, not as salvific atonement or substitutionary death at all; his radical message of justice and egalitarianism led to the cross. In Matthew and Mark, Jesus' death, somewhat difficult for Jesus himself too, is pictured as good sacrifice for "others." Here caution is that sacrifice of Jesus does not automatically mean penal substitutionary death of Jesus. On one hand, meaning of Jesus' death can be constructed in the context of different communities behind the Gospels. On the other hand, apart from the later communities' meaning of Jesus' death, cause of Jesus' death can be constructed in a more historical sense,

which means analyzing all aspects of life in the world ranging from politics to economy to religion.

Excursus: The Problem of Mel Gibson's Movie The Passion of the Christ

As for me, the biggest problem of the Gibson's movie *The Passion of the
Christ* seems to condone the social, political evil of violence and injustice, and be blind to the massive power of evil evident in such atrocious,
unspeakable torturing and murdering under the cover of a divine plan.
The movie reflects Mel Gibson's Jesus—his passion for a "Western" Jesus,
who comes to die and is punished instead of "me." The movie begins with
a quote from Isaiah's Suffering Servant Song: "But he was wounded for
our transgressions, crushed for our iniquities; upon him was the punishment that made us whole, and by his bruises we are healed" (Isa 53:5).
Taking the theme of the suffering servant and applying to Jesus, Gibson
colors his "Jesus" with "substitutionary death" (the so-called penal substitution theory) with much violence in the movie. The movie is full of
unnecessary, exaggerated torture with little information about the cause
of Jesus' death in a historical sense. For me, the movie turns very disap-
pointing because of the needless violence without raising the historical
question of why Jesus was killed. I just felt throughout the movie that
there should not be another Jesus, who receives enormous torturing and
injustice caused by the evildoers. Let us get straight on the cause of Jesus'
death. If Jesus' preaching of the kingdom of God (*basileia theou*) had been
accepted by people, he would not have been killed. Jesus was opposed
and executed by those who resent his message. Jesus' passion for God's
love and justice got him killed.

The cost of this movie is too high in the sense that people do not
reflect on such a power of evil in the form of violence, in the form of
politics, or in the form of daily lives of ordinary people. The movie's im-
pression was that "the more violence on Jesus, the holier Jesus is, and the
more thankful Christians feel because "our sins are paid back." But again,
in other contexts that I put here, the message of the movie turns different in one hundred eighty degrees turn, "There should not be another
Jesus of unjust suffering and death in this world." Such atrocious, sense-
less violence and suffering must disappear in our world. On the other
hand, we should acknowledge that this movie is not a historical movie
in the sense of what really happened but a theological story, directed

and interpreted by Gibson who follows a specific understanding or the meaning of Jesus' death. If someone too quickly responds to this movie as if this were a history *per se*, he or she evidently does not distinguish between history and theology.

Even this theological story, with a vicious or violent role of the Jews and the Romans, should not be related to all Jews in history. Of course, there were not all Jews involved in accusations against Jesus. There were good and faithful people like Mary, Jesus' mother, Mary Magdalene, disciples, and many nameless women who followed Jesus. Also, we cannot simply equate Jewish ancestors with Jewish people today and in history. So if any person does not distinguish between individuals and community, and between the past and the present, that person brings in impending dangers of inviting another Hitler to emerge on the scene. I reject such a naïve thinking or attitude of the historicization of the gospel story. As a whole, this movie must be viewed critically and/or with multiple dimensions of the texts involving Jesus' life and death.

Bibliography

Adamo, David, ed. *Biblical Interpretation in African Perspective.* Lanham, MD: University Press of America, 2006.

Akhmatova, Anna. "Lot's Wife." In *The Complete Poems of Anna Akhmatova,* translated by Judith Henschemeyer, 273–74. Brookline, MA: Zephyr, 2000.

Allison, Dale. "The Eschatology of Jesus." In *The Origins of Apocalypticism in Judaism and Christianity,* edited by John J. Collins, 267–302. New York: Continuum, 2000.

———. *Jesus of Nazareth: Millenarian Prophet.* Minneapolis: Fortress, 1998.

Bailey, Randall, Tat-Siong Benny Liew, and Fernando Segovia, eds. *They Were All Together in One Place? Toward Minority Biblical Criticism.* Atlanta, GA: Society of Biblical Literature, 2009.

Barnes, Michael. *In the Presence of Mystery.* Mystic, CT: Twenty-Third, 2003.

Barthes, Roland. "Theory of the Text." In *Untying the Text: A Post-Structuralist Reader,* ed. Robert Young, 31–49. Boston: Routledge & Kegan Paul, 1981.

Barton, John. *The Nature of Biblical Criticism.* Louisville, KY: Westminster John Knox, 2007.

———. *The Nature of Biblical Criticism.* Louisville, KY: Westminster John Knox, 2007.

Beardslee, William. "Poststructuralist Criticism." In *To Each Its Own Meaning: An Introduction to Biblical Criticisms and Their Application,* rev. and exp. ed., edited by Steven L. McKenzie and Stephen R. Haynes, 253–67. Louisville, KY: Westminster John Knox, 1999.

Birch, Bruce, and Walter Brueggemann, et al. *A Theological Introduction to the Old Testament.* Nashville, TN: Abingdon, 2005.

Blount, Brian, Cain Felder, Clarice Martin, and Emerson Powery, eds. *True to Our Native Land: An African American New Testament Commentary.* Minneapolis, MN: Fortress, 2007.

Borg, Marcus. *Conflict, Holiness, and Politics in the Teaching of Jesus.* Lewiston, NY: Edwin Mellen, 1984.

———. *The Heart of Christianity: Rediscovering a Life of Faith.* San Francisco: HarperSanFrancisco, 2003.

———. *Jesus: A New Vision.* San Francisco: HarperSanFranciso, 1987.

———. *Meeting Jesus Again for the First Time.* San Francisco: HarperSanFrancisco, 1994.

———, and N.T. Wright. *The Meaning of Jesus: Two Visions.* San Francisco: HarperSanFrancisco, 1998.

Brenner, Athalya, Archie Chi-chung Lee, and Gale A. Yee, eds. *Genesis: Texts @ Contexts.* Minneapolis, MN: Fortress, 2010.

Brown, Michael. *What They Don't Tell You.* Louisville, KY: Westminster John Knox, 2000.

Carey, Greg. *Sinners: Jesus and His Earliest Followers.* Waco, TX: Baylor University Press, 2009.

Carroll, John. "Luke." In *The New Interpreter's Bible,* 679–708. Nashville, TN: Abingdon, 2010.

Charlesworth, James, and Walter Weaver, eds. *Jesus Two Thousand Years Later.* Harrisburg, PA: Trinity, 2000.

Chilton, Bruce, and J. J. McDonald. *Jesus and the Ethics of the Kingdom.* Grand Rapids, MI: Eerdmans, 1987.

Clark-Soles, Jaime. *Engaging the Word.* Louisville, KY: Westminster John Knox, 2010.

Collins, John J. *The Bible after Babel: Historical Criticism in a Postmodern Age.* Grand Rapids: Eerdmans, 2005.

Coogan, Michael. *The Old Testament: A Historical and Literary Introduction to the Hebrew Scriptures.* New York: Oxford University Press, 2010.

Crossan, John Dominic. *The Birth of Christianity.* New York: NY: HarperCollins, 1998.

———. *The Historical Jesus: The Life of a Mediterranean Jewish Peasant.* San Francisco: HarperSanFrancisco, 1991.

———. *In Parables: The Challenge of the Historical Jesus.* New York: Harper & Row, 1973.

———. *Jesus: A New Revolutionary Biography.* San Francisco: HarperSanFrancisco, 1994.

Danker, Frederick William, Walter Bauer, William F. Arndt, and Wilbur Gingrich. *Greek-English Lexicon of the New Testament and Other Early Christian Literature.* 3rd ed. Chicago, IL: University of Chicago Press, 2000.

Davies, W.D. and Dale Allison. *The Gospel According to Matthew: Vol. III.* Matthew 19–28, ICC. London and New York: T & T Clark International, 1997).

Derrida, Jacques. "Différance." In *Deconstruction in Context: Literature and Philosophy,* edited by Mark C. Taylor, 396–420. Chicago: University of Chicago Press, 1986.

———. "Différance." In *Margins of Philosophy,* translated by Alan Bass, 1–27. Chicago: The University of Chicago Press, 1982.

———. *Negotiations: Interventions and Interviews, 1971–2001.* Stanford: Stanford University Press, 2002.

———. *Of Grammatology.* Translated by Gayatri Chakravorty Spivak. Baltimore: Johns Hopkins University Press, 1974.

———. *Positions.* Chicago: University of Chicago Press, 1982.

———. "The Villanova Roundtable." In *Deconstruction in a Nutshell: A Conversation with Jacques Derrida,* edited by John D. Caputo, 1–28. New York: Fordham University Press, 1997.

Dube, Musa. *Postcolonial Feminist Interpretation of the Bible.* St. Louis, MI: Chalice, 2000.

Ehrman, Bart D. *The New Testament: A Historical Introduction to the Early Christian Writings.* New York: Oxford University Press, 2000.

Fee, Gordon D. *New Testament Exegesis.* Louisville, KY: Westminster John Knox, 2009.

Felder, Cain Hope, ed. *Stony the Road We Trod: African American Biblical Interpretation.* Minneapolis: Fortress, 1991.

Fewell, Danna. "Reading the Bible Ideologically: Feminist Criticism." In *To Each Its Own Meaning: An Introduction to Biblical Criticisms and Their Application,* rev. and exp. ed., edited by Steven L. McKenzie and Stephen R. Haynes, 268–82. Louisville, KY: Westminster John Knox, 1999.

Fish, Stanley E. *Is There a Text in This Class? The Authority of Interpretative Communities.* Cambridge: Harvard University Press, 1980.

Frei, Hans. *The Identity of Jesus Christ: The Hermeneutical Bases of Dogmatic Theology.* Philadelphia, PA: Fortress, 1975.

Fowler, James. *Stages of Faith: The Psychology of Human Development and the Quest for Meaning.* New York, NY: HarperOne, 1995.

Gadamer, Hans-Georg. *Truth and Method.* New York: Seabury, 1975.

Gingerich, Mark. "The Church as Kingdom: The Kingdom of God in the Writings of Stanley Hauerwas and John Howard Yoder." *Didaskalia* 19.1 (2008) 129–43.

Grenholm, Cristina and Daniel Patte. "Overture: Reception, Critical Interpretations, and Scriptural Criticism." In *Reading Israel in Romans: Legitimacy and Plausibility of Divergent Interpretations*, vol. 1, edited by Cristina Grenholm and Daniel Patte, 1–54. Harrisburg, PA: Trinity, 2000.

Guest, Deryn, Robert E. Goss, Mona West, and Thomas Bohache, eds., *The Queer Bible Commentary.* London: SCM, 2006.

Gunn, David. "Narrative Criticism." In *To Each Its Own Meaning: An Introduction to Biblical Criticisms and Their Application*, rev. and exp. ed., edited by Steven L. McKenzie and Stephen R. Haynes, 201–29. Louisville, KY: Westminster John Knox, 1999.

Hauweras, Stanley. *Against the Nations: War and Survival in a Liberal Society.* New York: Winston, 1985.

———, and William H. Willimon. *Resident Aliens: Life in the Christian Colony.* Nashville: Abingdon, 1991.

Hiebert, Theodore. "The Tower of Babel and the Origin of the World's Cultures." *JBL* 126.1 (2007) 29–58.

Holladay, Carl. *A Critical Introduction to the New Testament: Interpreting the Message and Meaning of Jesus Christ.* Nashville, TN: Abingdon, 2005.

Iser, Wolfgang. *The Act of Reading: A Theory of Aesthetic Response.* Baltimore: Johns Hopkins University Press, 1978.

Lee, Dorothy Ann. "John." In *The New Interpreter's Bible*, 709–34. Nashville, TN: Abingdon, 2010.

Jeansonne, Sharon. "The Daughters of Lot, Victims of Their Father's Abuse." In *The Women of Genesis: From Sara to Potiphar's Wife*, 31–42. Minneapolis: Fortress, 1990.

Keck, Leander. *Who is Jesus? History in Perfect Tense.* Columbia, SC: University of South Carolina Press, 2000.

Keener, Craig. *The Historical Jesus of the Gospels.* Grand Rapids, MI: Eerdmans, 2009.

Kennedy, George. *New Testament Interpretation through Rhetorical Criticism.* Chapel Hill: The University of North Carolina Press, 1984.

Kim, Yung Suk. *Christ's Body in Corinth: The Politics of a Metaphor.* Minneapolis, MN: Fortress, 2008.

———. "Christianity in South Korea." In *The Cambridge Dictionary of Christianity*, 696–97. Cambridge: Cambridge University Press.

———. "Jesus' Death in Context." In *the Living Pulpit* 16.2 (2007) 11.

———. "A Lesson from Studies of Source Criticism: Contradicting Stories and Humble Diversity in Creation Stories (Gen 1–2)." *The SBL Forum* 5.9 (October 2007) http://www.sbl-site.org/publications/article.aspx?ArticleId=728.

———. "Lex Talionis in Exod 21:22–25: Its Context and Origin." *Journal of Hebrew Scriptures* 6.3 (2006) http://www.jhsonline.org/cocoon/JHS/a053.html.

———. "Rationale and Proposal for the Journal of Bible and Human Transformation." *Journal of Bible and Human Transformation* 1.1 (November 2011) http://www.

bibleandtransformation.com/JBHT/Volume_1_(2011)_files/JBHT%201%201%20 Kim.pdf.

———. "The Story of Hannah (1 Sam 1:11—12:11) from the Perspective of *Han*: The Three-phase Transformative Process." *The Bible and Critical Theory* 4.2 (2008) 26.1— 26.9 DOI:10.2104/BC080026.

———. "Teaching the Bible in a Different Culture." Teaching Theology in a Global and Transnational World (November 27, 2011) http://teachingtheology.blogspot. com/2011/11/teaching-bible-in-different-culture.html.

———. *A Theological Introduction to Paul's Letters.* Eugene, OR: Cascade Books, 2011.

Kristeva, Julia. *Revolt, She Said: An Interview by Philippe Petit.* Translated Brian O'Keefe. Los Angeles: Semiotext, 2002.

Lancaster, Sarah. *Women and the Authority of Scripture: A Narrative Approach.* Harrisburg, PA: Trinity, 2002.

Lévinas, Emmanuel. *Alterity and Transcendence.* Translated by Michael B. Smith. New York: Columbia University Press, 1999.

———. *Difficult Freedom: Essays on Judaism.* London: Athlone, 1990.

Liew, Tat-Siong. *What is Asian American Biblical Hermeneutics?* Hawaii: University of Hawaii Press, 2008.

Martin, Dale. *Pedagogy of the Bible.* Louisville, KY: Westminster John Knox, 2008.

———. *Sex and the Single Savior.* Louisville, KY: Westminster John Knox, 2006.

———. "Social-scientific Criticism." In *To Each Its Own Meaning: An Introduction to Biblical Criticisms and Their Application,* rev. and exp. ed., edited by Steven L. McKenzie and Stephen R. Haynes, 125–41. Louisville, KY: Westminster John Knox, 1999.

Martin, Gary. *Multiple Originals: New Approaches to Hebrew Bible Textual Criticism.* Atlanta, GA: Society of Biblical Literature, 2010.

McKenzie, Steven L,. and Stephen R. Haynes, eds. *To Each Its Own Meaning: An Introduction to Biblical Criticisms and Their Application.* Rev. and exp. ed. Louisville, KY: Westminster John Knox, 1999.

McKnight, Edgar. "Reader-response Criticism." In *To Each Its Own Meaning: An Introduction to Biblical Criticisms and Their Application,* rev. and exp. ed., edited by Steven L. McKenzie and Stephen R. Haynes, 230–52. Louisville, KY: Westminster John Knox, 1999.

Metzger, Bruce M., and Bart Ehrman. *The Text of the New Testament.* Oxford and New York: Oxford University Press, 2005.

Meeks, Wayne. *The First Urban Christians.* New Haven: Yale University Press, 2003.

———. "The Man from Heaven in Johannine Sectarianism." *JBL* 91.01:44–72.

Morgan, Donn. *Between Text and Community: The "Writings" in Canonical Interpretation.* Minneapolis, MN: Fortress, 1990.

Miller, Robert J., ed. *The Apocalyptic Jesus: A Debate.* Santa Rosa, CA: Polebridge, 2001.

Newsom, Carol and Sharon Ringe, eds. *The Women's Bible Commentary.* Louisville, KY: Westminster John Knox, 1998.

Odell-Scott, David. "Let the Women Speak in Church: An Egalitarian Interpretation of First Corinthians 14:33b-36." *Biblical Theology Bulletin* 13.3 (1983) 90–93.

———. "Editor's Dilemma." *Biblical Theology Bulletin* 30.2 (2000):68–74.

Palmer, Richard. *Hermeneutics: Interpretation Theory in Schleiermacher, Dilthey, Heidegger, and Gadamer.* Evanston, IL: Northwestern University Press, 1969.

Patte, Daniel. *The Challenge of Discipleship.* Harrisburg, PA: Trinity International Press, 1999.

———. *Ethics of Biblical Interpretation: A Reevaluation.* Kentucky: W/John Knox Press, 1995.

———. *The Gospel of Matthew: A Contextual Introduction for Group Study.* Nashville, TN: Abingdon, 2003.

———, ed. *Global Bible Commentary.* Nashville, TN: Abingdon, 2004.

———. "The Kingdom of God." In *Cambridge Dictionary of Christianity.* New York: Cambridge University Press, 2010.

———. "Structural Criticism." In *To Each Its Own Meaning: An Introduction to Biblical Criticisms and Their Application,* rev. and exp. ed., edited by Steven L. McKenzie and Stephen R. Haynes, 183–200. Louisville, KY: Westminster John Knox, 1999.

Pereboom, Derk. "Stoic Psychotherapy in Descartes and Spinoza." *Faith and Philosophy* 11 (1994) 592–625.

Powell, Mark. *Chasing the Eastern Star: Adventures in Biblical Reader-response Criticism.* Louisville, KY: Westminster John Knox, 2001.

Räisänen, Heikki. *The Rise of Christian Beliefs.* Minneapolis, MN: Fortress, 2009.

Reinhard, Kenneth. "Toward a Political Theology of the Neighbor." In *The Neighbor,* 71–73. Chicago, IL: University of Chicago Press, 2005.

Rhoads, David, and Donald Michie. *Mark as Story: An Introduction to the Narrative of a Gospel.* Philadelphia, PA: Fortress, 1982.

Risser, James. *Hermeneutics and the Voice of the Other: Re-reading Gadamer's Philosophical Hermeneutics.* Albany, NY: State University of New York Press, 1997.

Sakenfeld, Katherine. "Whose Text Is It?" *Journal of Biblical Literature* 127.1 (2008) 5–18.

Sanders, E. P. *Paul and Palestinian Judaism.* Minneapolis, MN: Fortress, 1977.

Santner, Eric. *On the Psychotheology of Everyday Life: Reflections on Freud and Rosenzweig.* Chicago, IL: University of Chicago Press, 2001.

Schleiermacher, Friedrich. *Schleiermacher. Hermeneutics and Criticism: And Other Writings.* Edited by Andrew Bowie. Cambridge, UK: Cambridge University Press, 1998.

Schneiders, Sandra. *The Revelatory Text: Interpreting the New Testament as Sacred Scripture.* Collegeville, MN: Liturgical, 1999.

———. *Written That You May Believe: Encountering Jesus in the Fourth Gospel.* New York: Herder & Herder, 2003.

Schüssler Fiorenza, Elisabeth. *In Memory of Her: a Feminist Reconstruction of Christian Origins.* New York, NY: Crossroad, 1994.

———. *Rhetoric and Ethic.* Minneapolis, MN: Fortress, 1999.

Schweitzer, Albert. *The Mystery of Kingdom of God: the Secret of Jesus' Messiahship and Passion.* London: A & G Black, 1925.

———. *The Quest of the Historical Jesus.* New York: Macmillan, 1968.

Segovia, Fernando F. *Decolonizing Biblical Studies.* Maryknoll, NY: Orbis Books, 2000.

———. "Reading the Bible Ideologically: Socioeconomic Criticism." In *To Each Its Own Meaning: An Introduction to Biblical Criticisms and Their Application,* rev. and exp. ed., edited by Steven L. McKenzie and Stephen R. Haynes, 283–306. Louisville, KY: Westminster John Knox, 1999.

———, ed. *Reading from This Place.* Vols. 1–2. Minneapolis, MN: Fortress, 1995 and 2000.

Segovia, Fernando, and R. S. Sugirtharajah. *Postcolonial Commentaries on the New Testament Writings.* London and New York: T. & T. Clark, 2009.

Sharp, Carolyn J. *Wrestling the Word*. Louisville, KY: Westminster John Knox, 2010.

Smith, Wilfred. *What is Scripture?* Minneapolis, MN: Fortress, 1993.

Soulen, Richard N. *Sacred Scripture*. Louisville, KY: Westminster John Knox, 2009.

Stassen, Glen, and David Gushee. *Kingdom Ethics*. Downers Grove, IL: InterVarsity, 2003.

Stendahl, Krister. "The Bible as a Classic and The Bible as Holy Scripture." *JBL* 103.1 (1984) 3–10.

Stott, Jack. *Decisive Issues Facing Christians Today*. London: Marshall Pickering, 1990.

Theissen, Gerd. *The Sociology of Early Palestinian Christianity*. Minneapolis, MN: Fortress, 1978.

Tamez, Elsa. "Women's Rereading of the Bible." In *Voices from the Margin,* edited by R. S. Sugirtharajah, 48–57. Maryknoll, NY.: Orbis, 1995.

Tolbert, Mary Ann. "Mark." In *The New Interpreter's Study Bible,* 1806, 1813–14. Nashville, TN: Abingdon, 2003.

Tov, Emanuel. *Textual Criticism of the Hebrew Bible*. Minneapolis, MN: Fortress, 2001.

Tracy, David. "Interpretation of the Bible and Interpretation Theory." In *A Short History of the Interpretation of the Bible,* 2nd ed., by Robert Grant and David Tracy, 153–66. Minneapolis, MN: Fortress, 1984.

———. "Theological Interpretation of the Bible Today." In *A Short History of the Interpretation of the Bible,* 2nd ed., by Robert Grant and David Tracy, 167–80. Minneapolis, MN: Fortress, 1984.

Trible, Phyllis. "Authority of the Bible." In *The New Interpreter's Study Bible,* 2248–2260. Nashville: Abingdon, 2003.

Vanhoozer, Kevin. "The Reader in New Testament Interpretation." In *Hearing the New Testament,* edited by Joel B. Green, 301–28. Grand Rapids: Eerdmans, 1995.

Wainwright, Elaine. *Shall We Look for Another: A Feminist Rereading of the Matthean Jesus*. Maryknoll, New York: Orbis, 1998.

Walker, William. "Kingdom of the Son of Man and the Kingdom of the Father in Matthew." *Catholic Biblical Quarterly* 30.4 (1968) 573–79.

Welborn, Laurence. *An End to Enmity: Paul and the Wrongdoer of Second Corinthians*. Berlin: De Gruyter, 2011.

———. "Paul and Pain: Paul's Emotional Therapy in 2 Corinthians 1.1–2.13; 7.5–16 in the Context of Ancient Psychagogic Literature." *New Testament Studies* 57 (2011) 547–70.

Westerholm, Stephen. "Matthew." In *the New Interpreter's Bible,* 635–38. Nashville, TN: Abingdon, 2010.

Wilder, Amos. *Theopoetic: Theology and the Religious Imagination*. Philadelphia: Fortress, 1976.

Wink, Walter. *The Human Being: Jesus and the Enigma of the Son of the Man*. Minneapolis, MN: Fortress, 2001.

Wire, Antoinette Clark. *The Corinthian Women Prophets: A Reconstruction Through Paul's Rhetoric*. Minneapolis: Fortress, 1990.

Wright, N. T. *Scripture and the Authority of God*. New York: HarperOne, 2011.

Yoder, John Howard. *The Christian Witness to the State*. Newton, KS: Faith and Life, 1964.

———. *For the Nations*. Eerdmans, 1997.

———. *The Politics of Jesus: Vicit agnus noster*. Grand Rapids: Eerdmans, 1972.

———. *The Priestly Kingdom*. Norte Dame Univ. Press, 1984.

———. *The Royal Priesthood*. Eerdmans, 1994

Žižek, Slavoj, Eric Santner, and Kenneth Reinhard. *The Neighbor: Three Inquiries in Political Theology*. Chicago, IL: University of Chicago Press, 2006.

Index

Hannah, 41n10, 43n11, 52n16, 55
Hauerwas, Stanley, 81n29
Haynes, Stephen, 17n12
heavenly home, 62
Hebrew scriptures, 12, 58–59, 78, 85
hedone, 48
Hellenism, 66
hermeneutical circle, 46
heteronomy, 53–55
hilasterion, 63, 91–92
historical critical, xiv, 15–18, 20, 23, 28–29, 31
historical Jesus, 66–67, 70n14, 80, 81n27, 85, 92
holism, 52, 89
holistic, 11, 52, 54–55, 69, 88–89
Holladay, Carl, 66n8, 71n15, 72n19, 74n20
Holy Spirit, 77
holy bible, 54
holy sacrifice, 62–63
homosexuality, 28
human dignity, 23, 47
human existence, 53–55, 59–60
human transformation, 14n3, 16, 36, 41n10, 80, 89
hypocrisy, 69, 72

identity, 8, 10, 19, 69, 74, 76–78, 82, 89
ideology, 20, 42, 50, 64
ideological criticism, 20
illusion, 22, 31
imagination, 45–46, 49, 59n2, 88
immortality, 61, 67
individualistic, 61
individuality, 53
inerrancy, 14, 45n1
interpolation, 3–4
inter-texts, 13
intertextuality, 16, 21
intervention, 37, 66, 80–81
Iser, Wolfgang, 19
Ishmael, 42–43, 50
isotes, 27

James, 63
Jeremiah, 64, 66–67, 92
Jews and Christians, 4, 14

Jewish war, 66
John (Gospel), 57, 61–62, 67, 69, 74–78, 90
Johannine community, 8–11, 69, 74
judgment, 30, 49, 61, 72, 81, 84, 91
justice, 1, 9, 11, 27–28, 30, 37, 42, 48–50, 61–64, 67, 71, 73, 78–84, 91–93
justification, 1, 5, 45n1, 61

kapporeh, 92
katalambano, 6–7, 12
Keck, Leander, 66n9
Keener, Craig, 66n9, 67n12, 70n14
Kennedy, George, 17n14
kenosis, 89–90
Kim, Yung Suk, 1n1, 4n5, 5n9, 9n14, 16n11, 21n27, 23n40, 28n3, 41n10, 46n3, 49n12, 59n2
kingdom of God, 12, 27, 46n4, 58–85, 87–90
kingdom of heaven, 68, 71–72
krino, 45
Lancaster, Sarah, 20n25
Last Supper, 70
Levinas, Emmanuel, 41n10, 89
Liew, Benny, 20n24
liberation, 10–11, 80, 82
literalism, 14, 17, 45n1
literary approach, 17
logocentrism, 21
logos, 7, 9–10, 62, 74–78
Lord's Prayer, 91
Lot, 62
Lot's wife, 20–21, 62
love and justice, 11, 49–50, 63, 84, 90, 93
low self-esteem, 51
Luke (Gospel), 30, 51, 66, 69, 72–74,
lype, 48–49

malkuth, 65, 85
Mark (Gospel), 66, 69–72, 92
Martha, 75
Martin, Dale, 2, 15, 17n13, 28–29
Martin, Gary, 5n8
Mary, 94
Macdalene, 94
Matthew (Gospel), 36–37, 68–73, 91–92